PORTLAND S
GREATEST
CONFLAGRATION

PORTLAND'S GREATEST CONFLAGRATION

THE 1866 FIRE DISASTER

DON WHITNEY & MICHAEL DAICY

WITH THE PORTLAND VETERAN FIREMEN'S ASSOCIATION & THE PORTLAND FIRE MUSEUM

Charleston · London

THE
History
PRESS

Published by The History Press
Charleston, SC 29403
www.historypress.net

Cover image: Looking west on Congress Street from Smith Street. *Painting by George Frederick Morse. Collections of Maine Historical Society.*

First published 2010

Manufactured in the United States

ISBN 978.1.59629.955.9

Library of Congress Cataloging-in-Publication Data

Daicy, Michael.
Portland's greatest conflagration : the 1866 fire disaster / Michael Daicy and Don Whitney
; with the Portland Veteran Firemen's Association and the Portland Fire Museum.
p. cm.
Includes bibliographical references.
ISBN 978-1-59629-955-9
1. Portland (Me.)--History--19th century. 2. Fires--Maine--Portland--History--19th century.
3. Disasters--Maine--Portland--History--19th century. 4. Fire extinction--Portland--
History--19th century. I. Whitney, Don. II. Portland Veterans Fireman's Association
(Portland, Me.) III. Portland Fire Museum (Portland, Me.) IV. Title.
F29.P9D34 2010
974.1'91--dc22
2010036877

This publication is dedicated to the Daicy and Whitney families for their patience and understanding during our many hours of research and energy fueled by our passion for the Portland Fire Department and this book.

Also to all past, present and future Portland firefighters who have saved countless lives and millions of dollars of property in this great city since 1768.

CONTENTS

PREFACE

The key turned in the lock as it had hundreds of times before. The big dark green door of the old engine house swung open and the curator stepped inside. The main floor was dark except for a single light on the alarm board. The faint outline of well-kept hand fire engines from the 1840s and 1850s could be seen. A large gleaming steam fire engine from the 1870s stood high at the rear. The singular light barely shined into the old fire alarm office, with its massive black slate circuit boards with brass fixtures. Highlights of the painted doors of the fire horse stalls were visible. Everything appeared to be in place. The main floor was in good order.

The curator decided to turn on the overhead lights and the spots directed onto the exhibits. Michael, the museum archivist, would be pulling in soon. He was collecting images for a new project. In his position as archivist, Michael was responsible for the care and exhibiting of hundreds of framed photographs. He worked for hours identifying photographs and building and maintaining archival files on more than fifty categories in two large file cabinets, which contain documents dating to the late 1700s and hundreds of ancient handwritten record books and logs from the Portland Fire Department and the individual fire companies. His duties include designing and building wall displays, performing microfilm research and the preservation of paper records, newspapers, film, audio tapes and discs. He spends countless hours each year here at the Portland Fire Museum. The least I can do, the curator thought, is turn on the lights for him.

The curator walked to the back of the main floor, passing the many leather fire buckets, the firemen's helmet shields in the case and the sections of leather fire hose. That hose was two and a half inches in diameter, a size established in the 1600s. The best cut of leather from the steer, when folded over to be hand stitched, came out to two and a half inches in diameter. The brass couplings were then made to fit the hose. In the decades of tours conducted through the Portland Fire Museum, the docents had related that story what seemed to be thousands of times.

Many of the guests were interested in that tale and the one about the leather fire buckets and the part they played in the colonial dating game. They also, during the tour, learned certain terminology of the history of firefighters and fighting fire, including terms like "bed key," "hogshead," "swob," "wattle" and "Higby cut."

The museum was the place to see thousands of firefighting-related accessions, and the members of the Portland Veteran Firemen's Association were always ready to run a tour through. There were true stories attached to each exhibit, some dating to the eighteenth century and some from the careers of the museum docents themselves, most of whom were Portland firefighters, either active or retired. Those who were not possessed an intense interest and knowledge in the history.

Michael is a member of Engine Company 11, a busy unit responding to 1,463 runs annually. The firefighter term "run" was coined in the 1700s when the firemen actually pulled the fire engines with ropes, running as a team. The engine companies of fifty to seventy men reported to their engine house upon an alarm and "got on the ropes." Then, on the order of the director—now known as the captain—they began the run to the fire. Today, the Portland Fire Department responds to more than 14,000 incidents. Citywide, that translates into 29,834 emergency movements of apparatus, or runs, annually.

The curator had retired from Engine Company 6. That company could trace its roots to the hand fire engine Vigilant, which was placed in commission in 1794. Previously, he had been assigned to Engine Company 4 for many years in the 1960s and 1970s, when the company ran from the quarters in Bramhall Square. Engine 4's former quarters were at 155–157 Spring Street, in the 173-year-old engine house now housing the Portland Fire Museum. As the curator hit the group of light switches that illuminate the main floor, he could almost picture the evolution of the firehouse.

The Hand Fire Engine Company, Ocean No. 4, had moved in just prior to the building's dedication in December 1837. The following years, it was home to not only Ocean 4 but also other hand engine companies, which were subsequently assigned to the West End. It was active as a hand engine house until Steam Fire Engine Company No. 4 was relocated from another section of the city, occupying the building during March 1874.

To accommodate the steam engine in the house, accompanied by a four-wheeled hose reel, the main floor was remodeled with the construction of stalls for the fire horses: large Percheron horses. There were six austere, sturdy stalls, each with double doors featuring windows and panels of the same herringbone design of the ceiling. The heavy steam fire engines worked out of the house, with the huge fire horses living in the stalls on the main floor and the firemen living on the second floor from 1874 to 1920. It was in 1920 that the steamer, wagon and fire horses were replaced by a single motorized double combination pumper, lettered in gold: "Engine 4." The double combination pumper was equipped with a 750-gallon-per-minute pump and a hose bed. This combined two functions that were previously separate horse-drawn units.

Various motor pumpers were assigned to the company through the years until June 1966, when the company moved into the new Bramhall Square Firehouse. The Spring Street building was vacated and closed. It remained so until 1975, when the Portland Veteran Firemen's Association was compelled to move from its quarters in another ancient engine house, which was to become a victim of urban renewal.

The Portland Veteran Firemen's Association had amassed a collection of fire memorabilia since its organizational meeting in 1891. The association held weekly meetings, and at each of those meetings many historical or fire-related relics were presented by citizens through the association's members and placed in display cases. These unsolicited contributions, from badges to fire engines, have continued to be received, up to the present monthly meetings.

When the association moved into the vacant Engine 4 firehouse, it also opened to the public, on July 4, 1975, under the name Portland Fire Museum.

The curator turned on the lighting in the cases. Of the men who were members of the hand engine company here, those of the next generations who cared for and handled the horses and operated the steam engines and the firefighters of the motor age who ran fire engines propelled and pumped by the internal combustion engine on a vehicle that carried hose and water, none thought he was making history. Their firehouse, though, is now filled with their stories, their photographs, their tools and equipment and the very apparatus with which they safeguarded the citizens and their property in the city of Portland. As a member of the Portland Veteran Firemen's Association, the curator, along with other firefighters and associate members, appreciated and protected the museum's hundreds of photographs and colored lithographs. Through these, they could show the guests what the firefighting apparatus and equipment and the individual firefighters looked like from early times to the first years of the twenty-first century.

Contained within the walls of the Portland Fire Museum is more history, up close and within reach, than one is able to absorb in a single visit.

Guests often inquire about the slide poles firemen use to quickly get to the main floor at the sound of an alarm or the red fire alarm boxes on the streets. They ask why, if it's a false alarm, do so many fire engines respond. The docents explain that it is an alarm of fire until the firefighters arrive and determine it to be a malicious false alarm. A prescribed number and type of fire apparatus are required to respond to fire alarm boxes in various sections of the city.

Visitors ask about an uncle or grandfather, or great-great-grandfather, who was once a Portland fireman. The docents are often able to take them to a photograph or portrait of their ancestors and sometimes locate examples of their handwriting. That's always a big hit.

The curator grabbed the wide dry mop and began walking it back and forth on the hardwood floor. As he worked, he thought about one of the most often asked questions: what about that big fire that burned Portland down? Most of the visitors know a bit about the event and are surprised to learn of the great extent of the fire, the destruction of a major segment of the city and of the place the fire holds in American history. The museum features an exhibit of framed photographs, taken on July 6, 1866, one day after the fire was extinguished. With sufficient familiar landmarks that remain standing, the devastation is crystal clear in each of the prints. Jagged remains of walls, chimneys, scorched trees and hundreds of collapsed buildings present a haunting scene.

The major permanent exhibit of photographs was taken by Boston photographer John A. Whipple. When he received word of the city of Portland being decimated by a large fire, he took his photographic equipment to the railroad station and boarded a train from Boston to Portland. At the time, he was unaware that the photographers' studios in Portland had been casualties of the conflagration. Whipple was noted for his photographs of buildings and cityscapes in Boston and other American cities. He was also distinguished for pictures and portraits of famous

Americans and their families. With a keen interest in the night heavens, Whipple received awards for his amazing and successful photographs of stars, taken through a telescope.

John Whipple arrived in Portland and, on a warm July 6, set up in the top of the burned-out Custom House building at Middle and Exchange Streets. From that vantage point, he was able to record the devastation in many directions. He then moved throughout the burned-out sections, at times photographing from street level.

The following week, on July 12, 13 and 14, Boston photographer John P. Soule left his downtown office on Washington Street and arrived in Portland to obtain his unique views of the fire's aftermath. He used the same vantage point of the Custom House and then set up his equipment at the top of the Portland Observatory on Munjoy Hill. The observatory had been built in 1807 by a group of shipping merchants to observe the harbor and signal the arrival of ships into port. A number of the merchants were Fire Wards or firemen who devoted years of their lives to defending the town from the ravages of fire. Ironically, now photographs were being taken from the top of their tower to record the wreckage from the most devastating urban fire in America. Soule issued his photographs as a set of stereoscopic views.

As the curator continued to push the mop across the shiny hardwood floor, he thought about how he and the docents relate vignettes and respond to the guests' questions, realizing the answers may often fall short concerning this particular vital catastrophe. They, as firefighters, would prefer to have the time to describe, in detail, the entire story.

ACKNOWLEDGEMENTS

The authors are grateful to those who have provided inestimable time, counsel, resources and courtesies in the development of this publication:

William David Barry, Maine Historical Society
Hilary Bassett, Greater Portland Landmarks, Inc.
Albert K. Bowers Jr., Principal Operator (ret.), Boston Fire Alarm
Dani Fazio, Maine Historical Society
Mr. Gary Goddard, Image Consultant
Greater Portland Landmarks, Inc.
Maine Historical Society
Edward Marks, President, Portland Fire Museum
Nicholas Noyes, Maine Historical Society
Michael Sanphy, Portland Veteran Firemen's Association
Earl G. Shettelworth Jr., Maine Historic Preservation Commission

ARTISTS:
George Frederick Morse, 1834–1925 (fireman Hydraulion HFE 8)
Charles Quincy Goodhue, 1835–1910 (fireman Tiger HFE 3)
Woodbury Hatch, 1829–1904 (fireman Volunteer HFE 3)

INTRODUCTION

C onflagration: a word that is often misused. There are fires, there are large fires and there are conflagrations. Even the National Board of Insurance Underwriters in 1917, a half century after its founding, still endeavored to define the word.

The National Board of Fire Underwriters was organized in April 1866. Following the July 4 and 5, 1866 Portland conflagration, the board's first annual meeting was held on February 20, 1867, to determine the risk of issuing fire insurance in cities. The National Board of Fire Underwriters was instituted to establish and maintain a uniform rate of premiums and to repress incendiarism and arson by combining, in suitable measures, apprehension, conviction and punishment. As such, the Board of Fire Underwriters was considered for decades the authority on fire protection, destruction and losses. Following the Portland conflagration, the number of fire insurance companies that paid out a large percentage of their holdings, or those that paid out and closed their doors forever, made clear the requirement to measure their risk and adjust rates accordingly by grading cities in regard to their fire defenses. The National Board of Fire Underwriters became the major fire prevention organization in the United States and is largely responsible for the National Building Code. In spite of the authoritative standing of the Board of Fire Underwriters, the definitive description of conflagration appeared to be elusive.

"Conflagration," from the Latin *conflagratio*, will be defined in this text as a fire that involves one or more buildings and then, through convection, radiation and/or conduction, jumps streets and blocks, involving many more buildings. A conflagration breeds its own heat and wind. These are so strong that they will oppose the natural wind. When a fire attains the huge magnitude of a conflagration, intense heat acts on massive amounts of ignitable construction or substances. The heat bakes out of materials partially consumed gasses, which readily burn when brought into contact with proportionate oxygen. In a conflagration, sufficient oxygen is often unavailable from surrounding air. The results are larger volumes of unburned combustible gasses at very high temperatures drifting with air currents. When masses of superheated gasses besiege a building, the heat will quickly break the windows; the gasses instantly enter the building and that fresh oxygen mixes to ignite in an almost explosive action. As the fire moves through the streets, sparks and brands are carried upward by hot-air currents, igniting more rising combustible gasses.

Following a conflagration, it's often heard that the "building burned within ten minutes" or "it erupted like an explosion." These statements are not exaggerations. Understanding the phenomenon of a conflagration, as explained above, we know that these descriptions are accurate.

From the first settlement of Falmouth Neck, which over the course of 368 years has evolved into the city of Portland, the area has experienced thousands of devastating fires, among them nineteen conflagrations. A tally of these conflagrations includes those in which the causes were either accidental, acts of battle or war or intentional:

1676	Falmouth Neck
May 15, 1690	Falmouth Neck
October 18, 1775	Falmouth
June 18, 1822	Green Street
October 12, 1842	Brown Street
June 2, 1845	Free Street
August 14, 1847	Cotton Street
January 9, 1849	Long Wharf and Maine Wharf
December 7, 1851	Commercial Wharf and Long Wharf
June 24, 1856	Temple Street
February 21, 1858	Head of Merrills Wharf
July 28, 1859	Fore Street and Franklin Street
July 4, 1866	68 blocks/1,500 buildings
August 25, 1870	Middle Street

February 5, 1890   Brown's Wharf, Berlin Mills Wharf, Marrott Wharf
                            and Merchant's Wharf
October 11, 1920   Boyd Street, Franklin Street and Oxford Street
October 22, 1961   Bishop Street and Mayfield Street
July 27, 1970   Grand Truck Railroad Wharf No. 7, Wharf No. 8
                            and Railroad Yard

In the cases of enemy attacks and the simultaneous setting fire to a number of buildings, the result would produce the same conflagration conditions. Each of these fires cited developed into a conflagration, primarily due to five factors that accompany most conflagrations:

1. The lack of sufficient water to effectively fight the fire.
2. The lack of sufficient fire companies quickly arriving and operating at the fire.
3. The lack of a sufficient number of firefighters working the early stages of the fire.
4. The presence of wind.
5. Delay in alarm.

In Portland, over its more than three hundred years, there were many fires that involved multiple buildings, from two to as many as twenty-nine at a time; however, because the fires did not reach the storm power of a conflagration, those are not included in this list.

The village, which grew into a town and then into a city, went through many hardships and setbacks, booms and depressions. In relating the story of the 1866 conflagration, an overview of the town's firefighting evolution must be examined to understand how the city of Portland arrived at the point of July 4, 1866, and witnessed the destruction of one-third of the city.

Writers and historians have long advanced their opinions about the great fire:

> *The fire started on the Portland waterfront while city firefighters were enjoying a holiday picnic at Sebago Lake.*[1]
> *Hoses weren't long enough to stretch to where the fire was burning.*[2]
> *Portland was greatly hampered by her fire department in trying to stop the conflagration. The department was an ill trained volunteer staff. At the start of the fire many companies and their equipment were attending the celebrations; They were not ready for an emergency.*[3]

Flames soon engulfed the building and spread to an adjoining one. Firemen easily extinguished the blaze and left.[4]

The firemen on account of their almost superhuman exertions were paralyzed and yet the wall of fire walked on—no check anywhere.[5]

Many have written, from as early as the week following the conflagration, of the firemen leisurely enjoying a picnic and not tending to duty in the city. These statements suggest an incrimination of the organization and members of the Portland Fire Department for the destruction of the major part of the city. This text will analyze the structure of the fire department, the control of City Hall, the era of transformation of the American fire service and man-made and natural events contributing to the conflagration.

Through news articles and books, the view of the Portland citizen is presented. Records of the firefighting officers and fire company members, some written in quill and ink, are recounted. Efforts of the firemen to improve the capabilities of fire protection will be noted, in their own words, as they requested and recommended appropriate apparatus and equipment to reduce the time between discovery of the fire and the application of water and the rescue of human life.

All are recurrent reminders of Winston Churchill's quote: "The farther back you look, the farther forward you can see."

FALMOUTH NECK

English settlers of this region first occupied Richmond Island off the coast of what are now known as the towns of Cape Elizabeth and Scarborough in 1628. The island was owned by Mr. Trelawny of Plymouth, England. Sixty men in his service dealt with the British ships, which loaded and transported fish, lumber and fur. Two men, George Cleeves and Richard Tucker, petitioned the provincial court to obtain a portion of the island for themselves. The decision of the court was a firm denial, and as a result, both Cleeves and Tucker were banished from the island. They and a small group of men in boats rowed from the island into the mouth of the harbor, landing on a point of land on the east end of a peninsula in 1632.[6] Native Abenakis knew the area as "Machigonne"; however, the settlers referred to the peninsula as a neck of land, so it became known as "the Neck."

The men built small homes of logs and clay with thatched roofs and wooden chimneys. They soon sent to the island for their wives and children. These families from England soon discovered that this was a region of extremes: winters with temperatures of well below zero and summers with days well above ninety degrees.

In 1658, the Massachusetts Colony, which controlled the territory, ordered that the extensive area now known as Portland, Westbrook, Cape Elizabeth, Falmouth, South Portland and Deering be designated as Falmouth, named in honor of a town in England at the mouth of the river Fal.

There were forty-two families in Falmouth Neck when Metacomet, Sachem of the Wampanoag tribe—more commonly known to the English as King Philip—went on the warpath in 1675. King Philip had witnessed too many malicious acts by the English upon his people and was intent on wiping out the towns and villages in the Northeast. During King Philip's War, Falmouth Neck was attacked and the crops burned. Some settlers escaped to the forest with their lives; however, thirty-four people were captured or killed by the braves, and every building in the settlement was destroyed by fire. In such an attack, there was no chance, and certainly no means of fighting the fire.

This was the first destruction of Falmouth Neck by fire.

THE SECOND CONFLAGRATION

Falmouth Neck was again settled following the signing of a treaty in 1678. As protection, Fort Loyal was built with most homes constructed in proximity. Although the six hundred villagers lived in harmony with the tribes, built mills, laid out streets and traded in lumber and fish, a second bloody war erupted in 1688. Known as King William's War, this was a result of the English failing to fulfill stipulations of the previous treaty. The war, which raged throughout New England, eventually involved the village of Falmouth Neck. In 1689, a war party of braves moved to the Neck for an attack. Before they reached the settlement, a fierce battle was fought on Brackets Farm,[7] where they were engaged by Major Benjamin Church of Boston accompanied by a troop of soldiers and sympathetic tribesmen. The battle lasted for seven hours, until the braves retreated into the forest. The timing of the appearance of the major, though unplanned, saved the village of Falmouth Neck.

Following the departure of Major Church to Boston, the war party returned months later in the spring of 1690, when a huge band of five hundred braves, reinforced and urged on by French soldiers, attacked. The onslaught at Fort Loyal lasted five grueling days and nights, until the men and boys were killed, the fort and all the buildings burned and the village again annihilated.

The settlers' corpses in the scorched remains of Fort Loyal, and in the dirt streets, broiled in the summer sun and froze in the winter ice for two long years, until the returning Major Church and his troops discovered and buried them.

This was the second destruction of Falmouth Neck by fire.

RECOLONIZATION

Resettlement began again in 1715. By 1728, many homes, mostly unpainted, were found on streets that were being developed from foot paths. Fore Street, Middle Street, Back Street and Center Street were the most heavily settled. Churches were built, as were wharves for the thirty vessels that called Falmouth home. Well-established shipping merchants owned fifteen sloops, seven schooners and various other boats and ships.

The first recorded fire occurred at Major Freeman's warehouse on February 26, 1753. The warehouse was lost due to the absence of an organized method of fighting fire. In this town, a serious fire, with no means to control or extinguish it, was devastating to the lives and economy of the citizens. With open hearths for heat, candles for light and wooden or clay chimneys with twigs to strengthen the clay, the threat of fire was always present. Chimney fires were dreaded. A fire in a chimney, with the igniting of creosote, disintegration of the dried clay and ensuing ignition of the sticks imbedded in the clay for strength, would produce a heavy, hot flame of ten feet blowing from the chimney. The resulting sparks and fire, carried by the ever-present breeze or wind from the harbor, rapidly involved the thatched roof and similar roofs of nearby buildings.

It was also a common practice to carry fire. To avoid attempting to start a fire in a fireplace with flint and shavings, fire was carried from the fireplace of one home to the fireplace of another home. The hazard was plain. The hot coals and fire being carried in a kettle would be fanned by the wind, and embers landing in brush or thatch immediately communicated fire to buildings. The means of disposing of refuse and dead brush in the village was by burning—another hazard that threatened the buildings. Stoves in ships moored at the wharves were easily overturned by the vessels' rocking movements, spilling fire onto the decks. The ships were soon involved in fires that extended to the dock and the buildings there. For all of these reasons, the threat of fire in Falmouth Neck was ever present.

In an initial attempt to defend the settlers against this threat, a town meeting was called on March 29, 1768. A very spirited, highly agitated gathering produced the organization that would protect Falmouth Neck against fire.

As ideas were presented and adopted, it was clear that every man, woman and child was expected to be involved in this vital protection. The effort of fire protection was supported and led by the merchants and business leaders. Not being content to let others do the work, they became deeply involved, with many accepting leadership positions. Rules addressing fire were drawn up by and for the citizens of Falmouth Neck:

1. Each household must have at the ready a certain number of leather fire buckets, equal to the number of chimneys on the house.
2. Each household must have raven duck bags measuring three feet by four feet with a drawstring. These bags were to be brought to the fire for the removal of goods from the burning building.
3. Fire Wards were appointed to patrol the Falmouth Neck streets after dark, to watch for fire and challenge anyone on the street after curfew.

Five men—Thomas Smith, Benjamin Titcomb, Benjamin Waite, Samuel Cobb and Enoch Moody—were appointed Falmouth's first Fire Wards. The Fire Wards carried a long staff as the emblem of office and a wooden ratchet-style rattle to sound the alarm upon the discovery of fire.

The authority granted to the Fire Wards required them to assume control at a fire. The responsibilities conferred upon these men amounted to them being the first fire chiefs and police officers of Falmouth Neck/Portland.

At the sighting of a fire, the wards would crank the wooden rattle, which, in the still streets of Falmouth, would echo loudly enough to awaken the citizens. The Fire Wards shouted the location—"Fire in Centre Street! Fire in Centre Street! Throw out your fire buckets!"—repeatedly until the citizens came running with their leather fire buckets in hand.

Recolonization

Upon the alarm of fire, all citizens were expected to respond and take up a position under orders of the Fire Wards. The Fire Wards would then order a line of men to handle the full leather fire buckets, hand over hand, from the water source—which may be a pond, a stream or the Fore River—to the burning building. Each bucket capacity was between one and one and a half gallons. About two hundred fire buckets would be used at a building fire. The water was thrown onto, or into, the fire building. For their efforts, only the most trivial of fires were extinguished. Much of the work was done to prevent nearby buildings from becoming involved in the fire.

The empty buckets were passed from the fire building back to the water source hand over hand by a line of women and children. The fire buckets never stopped in this continuous filling and application of water.

The lines of men and women were ordered by the Fire Wards to be formed back to back, with about four feet between the two formations. The wards wisely enforced this to prevent fraternization between the men and women and to keep strict attention to the work of fighting the fire. In the past, mothers of maidens were known to deliberately place their daughters in the line across from an eligible bachelor, to perhaps ignite another flame. The Fire Wards frowned on any such distraction at the fire scene and so implemented the back-to-back rule.

The Fire Wards possessed full control at the scene of a fire, including the power of arrest, in the case of looting or of an able-bodied citizen refusing to assist in fighting the fire.

ENJIN AND OPPOSITION

The subscribers to and delivery of the first fire "enjin"[8] in Falmouth Neck has not been documented. The enjin was presumably built in London, England, by Richard Newsham. He and his firm built many of the "water injins" being imported and employed in America. The pumper was a two-by four-foot box with carrying handles, a pump and an attached gooseneck nozzle. This was a crucial improvement over the direct application of water from the leather bucket. The buckets were filled, as previously described, from a water source, passed hand over hand and then emptied into the enjin. The men manipulated the pump handle, which forced the water into the pump, up through pipes into the gooseneck nozzle and was directed, under pressure, onto and into the fire building.

Newsham's enjins had been exported to America for many years. During this period of time, there were nine such enjins operating in Boston. The following entry from the *Records of the Town of Falmouth Neck*, confirms the existence of a pumper:

> At a legal *Town Meeting held in Falmouth on May 22ⁿᵈ, 1769, it was voted that Paul Little, William Owen, Jedidiah Cobb, Daniel Pettingill, Zebulon Noyes, Samuel Owen, Smith Cobb, Moses Plummer, Abner Lowell, Benj. Rand, Caleb Carter, Thomas Bradbury, David Bradish, John Rand and Peter Thomas and two others shall be excused from serving in any Town Office until March 1775, in consideration of their taking care of and managing the Engine to that time according to their Articles.*[9]

It is also indicated on an ancient map that a small building was constructed on Middle Street near King Street to accommodate the enjin.

By 1774, the population of Falmouth Neck had grown to two thousand. Many of those citizens were vocal and quite active in their opposition to British rule as early as 1766.

When the word of the Battle of Lexington reached Falmouth Neck, a large company of young men set out from the town destined for Cambridge. The despised English tax stamps, when delivered to Falmouth, were promptly seized by the citizens and burned in public. Of the unfairly imposed tea tax, the Patriots affirmed "that we will not buy or sell any India tea whatever."

This and other oppositions to the Crown were acknowledged on October 16, 1775, when Lieutenant Henry Mowatt of His Majesty's Navy, sailed his flagship and four other war vessels into the harbor.

A small party of British sailors rowed to the town and demanded that the citizens surrender their arms. This was not met well by the people of Falmouth, and "with loaded cannon pointed toward them, [they] resolutely rejected a proposition which carried with it the abject terms of surrendering their arms to save their property."[10]

October 18, at forty minutes past nine in the morning, shelling commenced. Heated cannon ball, grapeshot and shells, lasting for many hours, pummeling and igniting fires until finally ceasing at six o'clock in the evening.

In Lieutenant Mowatt's report, he stated:

> *At the same time, the cannonade began from all the vessels and continued till six—by that hour the body of the town was in one flame which would have been the case much sooner had the wind favored in the morning as it did in the evening: and although a regular cannonade was kept up all the time, numbers of armed men were employed extinguishing the fire before it became general which made it absolutely necessary for some men to be landed in order to set fire to the vessels, wharves, storehouses as well as to many parts of the town that escaped the shells and carcasses—not withstanding they were executed with the greatest dexterity.*

This party of British seamen returned to the town with torches and set fire to the remaining buildings, excepting about one hundred belonging to the Loyalists.

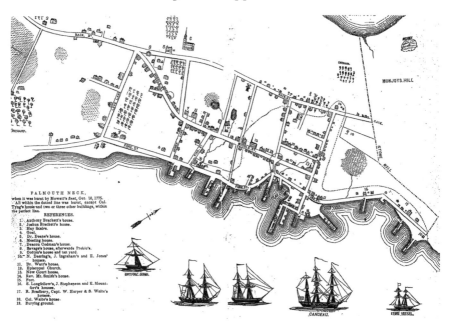

Map of Falmouth Neck (Portland) bombarded by Lieutenant Mowat's fleet of five vessels on October 18, 1775, during the Revolutionary War. A total of 414 buildings were burned. *Courtesy of Portland Fire Museum Collection.*

One of the first to be burned was the small enjin house in Middle Street, along with the enjin. Another 136 houses, the Anglican Church, the meetinghouse and the public library were also ignited by torches and destroyed. The total number of buildings burned was 414. In addition, eleven of Falmouth's ships were burned and sunk in the harbor, and 160 families were homeless with a vicious New England winter only weeks away. This was the third destruction of Falmouth Neck by fire.

LIBERTY AND REBIRTH

Extensive rebuilding over the next few years resulted in a recovering economy and improved living conditions. New streets were opened with new buildings. Fire protection was reorganized in 1783, when the Fire Society of Falmouth was formed. Thirty members provided themselves with canvas bags for salvage and leather fire buckets to be painted with the first letter of the given name and the surname at length (for example, E. Fernald).

Upon the alarm of fire, all members were to proceed to the member's house involved and preserve his effects. A watch word was whispered to the clerk at the fire, assuring that only members were protected by this form of insurance. In the case a member is suffering a loss, he may appeal to the Society, and may be given what the majority agrees to.

Following a long and bloody war of revolution, in 1783 America won independence from England. A movement was being developed by Falmouth Neck's most prominent citizens in 1785 to procure a fire engine by subscription. A notice appeared in the newspaper:

> The subscribers for a FIRE-ENGINE, are hereby notified to meet at the Meeting house on Monday next at ten o'clock in the forenoon, to choose a Committee to receive the sums that have been subscribed—and to give such Committee Instructions relative to the purchase of so useful a Machine. And as the sum already subscribed is not sufficient to procure one of so good kind as we wish to have—it is hoped that other persons who are desirous of promoting the design, would attend and contribute towards it.[11]

Falmouth Neck separated, on July 4, 1786, to become the Town of Portland, a name taken from a town in England south of Dorchester. Months later, after a wait of nearly two years, the fire engine arrived by sailing ship in Portland Harbor. On November 19, 1787, it was noted in the official record:

Agreeably to this warrant I have notified the inhabitants of said Portland to meet at the time and place to act upon the articles therin mentioned by posting up a copy thereof at two public places in said Town—At a legal meeting of the Inhabitants of Portland qualified to vote in town Meetings November 19th, 1787 Samuel Freeman Esq was chosen Moderator.

The subscribers for an Engine having voted "That the engine be presented to the town, the town agreeing to pay what is yet due for it; providing a house to keep it in; and taking care of it in all respects as a Town Engine; which being laid before the Town it was Voted That the town accept of the said Engine on the terms mentioned in the vote of said Propriations—Voted That the Select men be directed to build an engine house; and appoint Engine men as by Law empowered—Voted that this meeting be adjourned to 3 o'clock this afternoon at the office of S Freeman Esq";

The engine was two by four feet in size and was pulled through the streets by hand. It may have been equipped with wheels, although a passage regarding an alarm response describes the pumper as being placed on a wagon. A small wood-frame barn was erected, a crew was organized and the name "Neptune" was given to the "mashine."

The engine men were appointed annually by the selectmen:

Their duty is to meet together once a month, and oftener if necessary, for the purpose of examining the state of the Engine, and the appendages belonging to the same and feeling that the said Engine is in good repair, and ready to proceed on any emergency, to the relief of any part of the community that may be invaded by the calamity of fire—to go forward, either by night or by day, under the direction of fire wards, and to use their best endeavors to extinguish any fire that may happen in the town, or the vicinity thereof, and shall come to their knowledge, without delay. They are exempted from common and ordinary military duty, and from serving as Jurors, or in the office of a Constable, during the time they may be employed in service.[12]

William Farrington, Nathaniel Moody, Apollos Cushing, Enoch Morse, Richard Gooding, Joseph Weeks, John Clough, Hosea Illsley, John Emmons, Francis Chase, William Moody, John Lowel, Daniel Cobb, Thomas Beck and Joshua Rogers were the first so appointed.

From the preceding excerpts from newspapers and official records, it is apparent that the greatest attention and preparation were necessary to merely purchase and operate a fire engine.

In 1794, a second engine was built in London and shipped to Portland. This hand engine was named Vigilant and was built by Richard Newsham, at a cost of £100.

Buildings throughout the town were being built of both wood and brick, and by 1800 fine brick mansions were placed in the better locations of the town, with grand views of the harbor and islands. With increased construction of homes, shops, warehouses and wharves, the number of fire companies expanded out of necessity. Not only did the potential for destructive fire exist, but the actual incidents also occurred.

The following excerpt comes from a June 1, 1800 Portland newspaper:

> *A large new two story building at the head of Middle Street was entirely consumed last Friday. The owner, Mr. Isaiah Hacker and his family were at dinner upstairs, and some shavings on the hearth on the first floor caught and were blown around the room. The fire moved so fast the family had to be rescued. Loss to the building and contents were suffered by Mr. Hacker, the store of J&R Horton and Mr. Breed, a resident. The citizens worked to save the adjacent property and buildings.*

The town's expansion made the alarm of fire more difficult to transmit clearly. The cry of "Fire!" was still used with the location and street name, but it took longer to be repeated in all corners of the town. This situation was addressed in 1801. Fort Sumner was located on North Street overlooking the town with a commanding view of the harbor and Back Cove.

On February 21, 1801, the following "Notice of Fire" was issued:

> *The Selectmen of this town give notice, that on application to Captain Henry, commander of Fort Sumner, he has politely engaged to give orders to the Sentinel placed there and at the Battery, that if a Fire should be discovered to break out in the town at any time between eleven o'clock in the evening and four in the next morning, they discharge a six pounder*

*pointed towards the town to alarm the inhabitants; and also give immediate
information to Mr. Fernald and Mr. Burns that they may ring the bells for
the same purpose.*

An order was sent to London for a third hand fire engine in 1801. This
was an unusual barrel suction–style hand engine built by Joseph Bramah.
The engine arrived by sailing ship on February 11, 1802. It was designated
with the name Cataract by its crew. The men admired the large new pumper,
although they disapproved of the unexpected green color. After a vote, they
went to work having the pumper repainted vermillion, a brilliant scarlet
red. With its barrel-like silhouette, this earned the engine the nickname
"the old lobster."

This engine was much larger and heavier than any previously in town and
required a crew of seventy-nine men to pull it on a run and pump at a fire.

The following appeared in a Portland newspaper on July 9, 1805:

*The alarm of fire last night, for the head of Union Wharf. Storehouses
1,2,3, and contents were destroyed along with a shop occupied by Mr.
Woodman, hatter, and one by Mr. Hadley, blacksmith. Losses were
sustained by Captain Davis Smith, Hon. Woodbury Storer and Robert
Boyd who lost their stores and contents. Cause of the fire was suspected
to be smoking cigars in the sail loft above the stores. Caution against the*

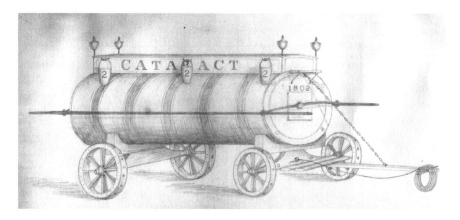

Drawing by C.Q. Goodhue of the Cataract Hand Fire Engine No. 2, built in England
in 1801. The engine was on display in City Hall's basement and destroyed in the
conflagration. *Courtesy of Portland Fire Museum Collection.*

fashionable nuisance. The citizens showed energetic efforts saving the wharf and many adjacent buildings from destruction. The tide was too low to provide access to water. The engines were seasonably on the spot and their crews worked hard. The Fire wards deserve public gratitude.

Another newspaper reported on January 18, 1808:

Yesterday at 7:50, the alarm of fire for Hay Market Row. A chamber fire over the third store from the west end on the brick row building. The rooms were occupied by printers offices and the presses were destroyed.

The fire moves west to the adjacent building and store of Mr. John Collins, then to the large store of Mr. Benjamin Willis. The fire moved until it reached the end of the uppermost block of buildings where a brick wall stopped the fire. The brick buildings remain standing, but five stores and two dwellings are destroyed. One small building was pulled down to stop the fire.

The following excerpt is from the March 30, 1819 *Portland Gazette*:

Alarm of fire on Friday 10:15pm, for a bake house on Fore Street. The fast moving fire trapped the family of Benjamin Bailey. The youngest children narrowly escaped with their lives. The older children in another room were burned to death. The wind pushed the fire to a two story brick building. The enginemen cut off the fire, although the building was damaged. Fire extended to Portland Pier to two buildings which were destroyed.

These reports of fires were common in the newspapers and fire log books. Each year, more property was damaged or destroyed by these frequent fires. The pulling down of buildings was necessary to stop the progress of fire by removing the fuel. The decision to order the removal of a building was not taken lightly and required the agreement of a number of Fire Wards before the order was given. The hooks and ladders were hung on certain buildings in the town, exclusively for use at a building fire. Men handled the large iron hooks with poles, ropes and chains. It was quite a feat.

The hook was attached to the end of the wooden pole and then raised to the roof and grappled firmly. The chain, bolted permanently to the hook, hung down to the street. The rope was fastened to the chain, which permitted many men to grasp the length of it. The fire ward would give the order to the ladder company foreman, who would shout, "On three, men!"

and then count down. The strain on the rope and hook would eventually pull the building apart. All of this took place as the fire continued to extend toward them—or over them.

The loss of any life as a result of fire is dreadful, and when the victims are children, the tragedy is compounded. These fires not only affected the firemen but also the citizens of the entire town. Everyone knew their neighbors and their neighbors' children.

The expansion of the town made the availability of ladders, and the running of them to the fire, more difficult. Some ladders used in Portland and throughout New England specifically for fire were wooden, single section and quite narrow. Others were of the fruit picking or "A" style of less than ten feet in length.

The ladders were hung on the side of certain buildings in the town and used only for fighting fire. A fine was imposed for the removal of a ladder for any other purpose.

It was necessary in 1827 to provide a hand-drawn carriage for the organization of a hook and axe company. The hooks, previously hung on centrally located buildings, were now secured on this carriage to be run quickly to the fire. The ladders were laid on the carriage along with axes and chains.

Considering the increasing population and size of the Town of Portland, it was recognized that a restructuring of the firefighting force must be implemented. A bill was written and submitted to the legislature.

PORTLAND FIRE
DEPARTMENT

The state legislature enacted a law effective on February 19, 1831, that established the Portland Fire Department. With this legislation came a new organization:

An act establishing a Fire Department in the Town of Portland; Approved February 19, 1831.

> *Sect. 1 Be it enacted by the Senate and House of Representatives, in Legislative assembled. That the Fire Department of the town of Portland shall hereafter consist of one Chief Engineer and as many other Engineers, Fire wards, Fire men, Hose men, Hook and Ladder men, Axe and Sail men as the Selectmen of said town from time to time, may nominate and appoint, not exceeding three hundred in addition to the number at present employed.*

> *Sect. 2 Be it further enacted, That it shall be the duty of the Engineers, or Fire Wards, to see that all the fire apparatus, belonging to said town, be constantly kept in good and complete order, and it shall be their duty to see that all Engines, Hose and Ladders, be cleaned and repaired as soon as may be after any fire.*

> *Sect. 3 Be it further enacted, That the Chief Engineer, Engineers, or Fire Wards so nominated and appointed shall have the same power and authority, relative to the pulling down or demolishing a house or other buildings to prevent the spreading of fires, also relative to all other matters and things affecting the extinguishment or prevention of fires, or the*

commanding assisting, as Fire Wards now by law have. And the said town of Portland shall be liable to pay all such reasonable compensation for damage done by, or consequent upon the acts or directions of said Chief Engineer, Engineers, or Fire Wards, as other towns in this State are liable to pay, in like cases, for damage consequent upon the Acts or directions of their Fire Wards.

Sect. 4 Be it further enacted, That the members of said Fire Department shall be liable to all the duties and shall enjoy all the privileges that other firemen in this State, are subject to and enjoy by law at the present time.

Sect. 5 Be it further enacted, That after the acceptance of this Act by the inhabitants of the said Town of Portland, the Selectmen shall be authorized and directed to make and publish such rules and regulations for the government and direction of the several members of the same as they may from time to time think proper and expedient; and the rules and regulations so made and published shall be binding upon the members of said Department and upon the inhabitants of the town generally, Provided, They shall not be contrary to the Constitution of this State and the provisions of the Act.

Sect. 6 Be it further enacted, That from and after the organization of a Fire Department under this Act, and notice thereof given in one or more newspapers published in said town by the Selectmen thereof, all laws of this State relating to the election of Fire Wards, so far as they affect the nomination and appointment of Fire Wards within said town, be and the same are hereby repealed.

Sect. 7 Be it further enacted, That the provisions of this Act shall not take effect until the same shall have been accepted by a vote of the town of Portland, taken by ballot at a general meeting called for that purpose.

This reorganization brought a more authoritative and organized system to Portland's fire protection, with the first chief engineer, Nathaniel Mitchell, and four assistant engineers. In the following months, a city charter was granted to the Town of Portland in 1832, establishing by law the City of Portland. Among the rules and regulations adopted by the Portland Fire Department on August 23, 1832, was Article 11: "It is recommended to the officers and members of the Engine and other companies, to prefect themselves in their several duties, by drills, as often as convenient."

The chief engineers recognized the vital importance of training for firemen. The ladder company instituted in 1827 was reorganized in 1831.

Drawing of Casco Hand Fire Engine No. 1, built by Stephen Thayer of Boston in 1835. Behind the engine are the engine company members in their uniforms. *Courtesy of Portland Fire Museum Collection.*

Washington Hook and Ladder Co. No. 1 was provided with a new truck, built in the city, and equipped with the necessary equipment. On the alarm, nine hand engines, a hook and axe wagon and a ladder carriage were run to the fires. With the establishment of the Portland Fire Department, fewer appointments of Fire Wards were made. The remaining wards worked in unison with the chief engineers until the expiration of their terms in 1837 and the elimination of the position.

The last fire ward was honorably discharged in 1837, and the improved organization of the Portland Fire Department was commanded solely by a chief engineer. The number of assistant engineers was authorized to be increased to 10. From 1768, when the wards were first appointed, to February 15, 1837, and the approval of the revised rules and regulations that eliminated the position of fire ward, 174 men had been appointed Fire Wards, from 5 to more than 30 annually, to serve and safeguard the town. Some men served in that office for many years.

By 1839, the city of Portland was protected by nine hand fire engine companies, two hose companies, two ladder trucks and five fire companies, which were organized to conduct salvage and protective work. The hand fire engines required companies of fifty or more men. The total number of firemen was about seven hundred men, according to Chief Engineer Neal Dow. It was Chief Dow, more than any of his predecessors, who brought a regimental tone to the operation of the fire companies.

These fire companies, consisting of elected members from all walks of life, were the social starting point for some notable figures of history. Each company adopted a distinct uniform for parades and special occasions. Hand Engine Company Ocean 4 wore red shirts and green trousers and caps. For the dirty work of fighting fire, oil skins were provided by the town. The uniforms, company songs and social side of being a fireman resulted in high morale within the companies.

Membership in the fire companies was the stepping-off point for some of the Portland firemen who later became well known for other ventures.

The aforementioned Neal Dow of Deluge Hand Engine Co. No. 7 served in the Union army during the Civil War as a colonel and was, in later years, nominated by the Prohibition Party for the office of president of the United States. Others of note were George Fredrick Morse of Hydraulion Hand Fire Engine No. 8, artist; Nathan Cleaves of Hose Co. No. 1, attorney and Civil War officer; Woodbury Hatch of Volunteer Hand Fire Engine Co. No. 3, noted artist; Daniel H. Chandler of Hose Co. No. 1, musician and band leader; Herman Kotszchmar of Hose Co. No. 1, classical musician and composer; Andrew T. Doyle of Hand Fire Engine Deluge No. 7, U.S. postmaster under President Lincoln; and John B. Brown of Deluge Hand Fire Engine No. 7, Portland sugar baron.

There were men who were later elected mayor of Portland, including William Senter of Deluge No. 7, William W. Thomas of Alert Hand Fire Engine, Jedediah Jewett of Casco Hand Fire Engine 1, Neal Dow of Deluge No. 7, J.B. Cahoon of Vigilant and Levi Cutter of Extinguisher Hand Fire Engine.

Portland is a hilly city on a peninsula that is approximately three miles long with an average width of three-quarters of a mile. At each end of the peninsula is a hill. To the northeast, Munjoy Hill, named for George Munjoy, an early settler, rises 160 feet above sea level. Bramhall Hill, named for tanner George Bramhall, is 175 feet high to the southwest. The low point between the hills measures 57 feet above the water. With this topography, the firemen were usually pulling the engines up a hill or down a hill. The hand tubs were built of iron, wood, brass and copper, making them very heavy. In the winter, snow was often above the hubs. The crews that pulled the enjin to the fire, set up the suction hose at the water source and ran the leather lead hose to attack the fire also pumped the engine. The pumping was at the rapid pace of roughly one stroke per second. This proved so demanding after a long run with the tub that some firemen would pass out from exhaustion.[13]

On appointed dates selected by their officers, engine companies would meet at the engine house to "break 'er down," the term used for pumping and in this case meaning a company drill. The firemen would get on the ropes as if they were responding to an alarm or a "run."[14] They would head to one of the sixteen reservoirs with the men on the hose reel laying out the leather leading hose in the street, a process that took about one minute. The leading hose was the leather hose that was stretched, or "led," into the fire building to attack the fire.[15] Within two minutes, the men on the engine connected the hard suction hose to the intake port of the engine and set the "brakes," the long wooden handles. The leading hose was connected to the discharge port of the engine, and the men got around the hand tub to handle the brakes. At the order of the foreman—"Atlantic Two! Pump away!"—the men, ten on each side, pumped the brakes up and down, action that forced, or drafted, the water from the reservoir into the pump, at pressure, out through the leading hose.[16]

The pumping by men on the left and right sides of the tub—or on some models, the front and rear of the tub—would be at a rate of one stroke per second, with the foreman shouting a cadence through a speaking trumpet to keep the men in rhythm.

This was fatiguing work, even for those who were in the best condition. "Break 'er down boys! Break 'er down!" the foreman would order to embolden and energize his crew. At times, the cadence was in the form of a chantey or poem written especially for the company.

These drills were training for the firemen to be at their best when responding to an alarm and operating at a fire. Following an hour or more of drilling, and after gathering a sizable crowd of spectators who watched and cheered them on, the order was given to "make up the line." The hose and equipment were drained and placed back on the reel. The next order was then given: "Atlantic Two! Limber up!" This order was for the men to get on the ropes and run the piece back to quarters.

A member of the Casco Hand Fire Engine Company, William Goold, writer and historian, related the following in a newspaper interview thirty years after that company's 1835 organizing:

> *It will seem ludicrous to the younger readers to think of these old grey headed fathers of the town and grandfathers of the boys old enough to run with the machine now, then ran to fires, dragging the engine through the mud of streets unlighted excepted by their own torches, crying "there goes*

No. 9, head her off!" "Here comes Neal Dow's double decker, let's run her out of sight"; "Hi-yah!" "Jump her!" "Jump her!"

The traditional green, the chosen color of the old rifle corps, was carried ahead of the engine, as a rallying signal, in the shape of a green lantern with No. 1 on it. The company wore black leather caps with a metal rib over the crown to prevent any one getting a brick in his hat. To the caps were attached rubber capes reaching to the waist. My own fit out as a leading hose man in addition to the cap and cape was a rubber coat and rubber boots and pants in one piece fastening with belt. On this belt was a small bulls eye lantern to give light in dark passages, and to admit the using of both hands.

I have the lantern yet. It was a present from a Boston fireman. With this rig one could stand on a ladder, with the hose hooked to a strap over his shoulder and the water pouring off the roof directly upon him for an hour, and come out dry. I recollect an hour's experience of this kind on the attic stairs of the old Dr. Porter house, on the East corner of Free and Center streets, which was on fire in the attic. Then, there was a sharp competition to see which engine would get the first water on, which prevented the fires

Atlantic Hand Fire Engine No. 2, built by Leonard Crockett of Portland in 1848, pumped at the July 4 conflagration. The engine survives as part of the Portland Fire Museum's collection. *Photograph by Michael Daicy.*

Portland Hand Fire Engine No. 5, built by Leonard Crockett in 1851, model by George Frederick Morse of Hydraulion Hand Fire Engine No. 8. *Courtesy of Maine Historical Society.*

getting much start before they were put out. It was a very rare thing for a fire to spread to the second building.

From 1837 to 1862, the Portland Fire Department responded to hundreds of alarms of fire. Many of these fires involved a building or a group of buildings. During that period, 230 buildings were severely damaged or destroyed. Of those 230 serious fires, many involved multiple buildings, and at some alarms, as many as 10 buildings were involved.

By 1847, the Portland Fire Department was organized as follows:

Chief engineer
Six assistant chief engineers

Hand Fire Engine Co. Casco No. 1	51 men
Hand Fire Engine Co. Cataract No. 2	no assigned co.
Hand Fire Engine Co. Volunteer No. 3	53 men
Hand Fire Engine Co. Ocean No. 4	50 men
Hand Fire Engine Co. Portland No. 5	58 men
Hand Fire Engine Co. Deluge No. 7	45 men
Hand Fire Engine Co. Hydraulion No. 8	46 men
Hand Fire Engine Co. Niagara No. 9	51 men
City Hose Co. No. 1	8 men
City Hose Co. No. 2	10 men
America Hose	no assigned co.

Bucket Carriage	no assigned co.
Washington Ladder Co. No. 1	20 men
Ladder 2	14 men
Ladder 3	no assigned co.
Total firemen and officers	406
Total chief engineers	7

Proper maintenance of the fire department was crucial to the economy and livability of the city. In 1858, the method of the alarm was improved. The town was divided into ten numbered districts. Upon the discovery of fire, the street and district number were shouted repeatedly by the one who discovered the flames. The cry was repeated by all who heard it until the church sextons began ringing the alarm. The district number was rung on the bells of Union Church and St. Stephen's Church. The district number was repeated following a brief intermission as many times as necessary. All other church bells tolled continually, giving the alarm.

The hand fire engines and the companies of men were quite effective. Many buildings in which fires occurred remain occupied today as a testimonial to the firemen's dedication, speed, courage and efficiency in fighting fire.

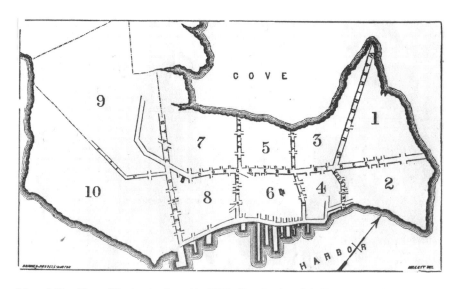

Map of Fire Alarm Districts instituted in 1858. Certain church bells were struck several times with the Fire District's number. *Courtesy of Portland Fire Museum Collection.*

The companies responded to an alarm on a cold night on January 4, 1856, for a fire in the building of Barker and Dingley Stables on Temple Street. The fire extended to the Temple Street Church as the firemen struggled in extremely frigid temperatures. The fire then jumped the street to the Codman House and the Casco House, two large, occupied hotels. It soon involved several other buildings occupied by stores, offices and dwellings. The loss amounted to $80,000.

On October 21, 1857, trials were conducted for the engine companies. Under the direction of the chief engineer, each engine company was to start the run on India Street and head up Fore Street to the Portland Company, which was one-quarter of a mile uphill, draft water through three lengths of suction hose and play through three hundred feet of leading hose into a hogshead of 160 gallons. This measured the engine company's pumping capability.

The trial, or drill, was another part of the firemen's training. The skills of working as a team, following orders, speed, efficiency, positioning the apparatus and handling the hose and equipment were all brought into play, with the added pressure of the other eight companies of firemen and the

Drawing of Portland City Hall, built in 1858, as it looked before it was destroyed on July 4, 1866. *Courtesy of Maine Historical Society.*

citizens watching. As an incentive, the company with the best times was presented with a beautiful ceremonial speaking trumpet, which it held until the trials the following year. The annual fire department budget was $7,931.83, of which firemen's pay was $3,800.00. The Portland firemen were not volunteers; they were paid per alarm answered. New oilskin suits were purchased for the firemen in 1858 at a cost of $112.50. These were for protection in fighting fire.

Twenty-six hand fire engines had been purchased by 1858, either privately, by subscription or by the Town through taxes over the ninety years of Portland's firefighting history.

STEAM AGE

In 1859, on October 7, the first steam fire engine was placed in service in the city. The pumper arrived in the city by train on October 1. On the fourth, the *Eastern Argus* reported:

> *The Steam Fire Engine Machigonne was tried yesterday afternoon in the presence of the members of the City Council and the Fire Department and an immense crowd of spectators. She drafted her water from the dock near Central wharf. In five minutes after the match she had on 10 lbs. of steam and the machine began to operate, throwing two separate one inch streams through 100 feet of hose. In ten minutes these streams were thrown far above the four storied granite building of Messrs. John Lynch & Co.—the steam gauge indicating 55 lbs. The next trial was a one inch and a one and a quarter inch nozzle, through the same length of hose. The streams were thrown as high as handsomely as those from the one inch nozzles. Subsequently other trials were made with a seven eighth of an inch nozzle, and throwing the streams horizontally. All of the performances gave satisfaction to those who witnessed it, and everyone was satisfied that she would be a most valuable auxiliary in case of fire. A second trial is to be made today.*

Machigonne Steam Fire Engine Co. No. 1 was quartered at 557 Congress Street near Oak Street.

The steam fire engine required a company of men numbering fifteen. It could pump more water for a longer time than the hand fire engines. In the

Machigonne Steam Fire Engine No. 1, built by Amoskeag of Manchester, New Hampshire, in 1859. The steamer and the engineer were quartered in the Congress Street Engine House, near Oak Street. *Courtesy of Portland Fire Museum Collection.*

case of the first steamer, it was capable of pumping nine hundred gallons per minute. The pumping capacity of the hand fire engines was not usually measured in gallons per minute but in the distance a stream of water could be thrown from the nozzle. A powerful hand engine was able to produce a stream of two hundred feet.

A new hose carriage was also delivered and equipped with new leather hose and tools. The steam fire engine companies, like the hand fire engine companies, were tandem companies with both a pumper and hose cart, carriage or wagon. The driver handled the engine, with a stoker on the back step feeding coal into the fire box with a shovel. The hose carriage was assigned a driver and, if large enough, was able to carry the engine company crew.

For each steam fire engine in commission, two hand fire engines were decommissioned, and for each of those, the sixty-man crew was honorably discharged from duty. That was the case on July 16, 1860, when Hand Fire Engine Companies Deluge No. 7, Casco No. 1 and even a third unit,

Hydraulion No. 8, received an order from the city board of aldermen notifying them to disband.

The first steam fire engine was appropriately christened Machigonne No 1. The engineer was the first appointed in the history of the Portland Fire Department. The term "engineer" referred to the training and responsibilities of the appointee to operate the steam engine and its pumps. The title is at times confused with that of the head of the fire department, known as chief engineer. The title chief engineer was adopted in 1831, since, as the commander of the department, he organized and directed, or *engineered*, its operation.

Edward W. Porter, the former foreman of Hand Fire Engine Company Pacific No. 9, had a background as a machinist with the Portland Company on Fore Street and was suited for the position of steam engineer. As such, he was the first paid, full-time fireman in the Portland Fire Department. At twenty-seven years of age, he was in charge of the steamer and kept the engine house at 557 Congress Street, near Oak Street, in top condition. He maintained the engine, as well as the hose reel carriage and the premises.

Porter could have been the most celebrated fireman in the city, considering his prominent position in this giant step in fire protection. Instead, he became the object of ridicule and, at times, violence, with certain members of the public stoning him and the massive steam fire engine. At one time, a mob burst into the Machigonne No. 1 engine house and was able to pull the engine out through the big doors, dragging it by rope up to Green Street and down the hill. The mobsters took the steamer to a bluff with the intention of dropping it over the rocks. Charles B. Nash, a member of Machigonne No. 1, received word of the affair and dashed to the bluff on Green Street, where the pumper was positioned precariously. Nash managed to sidle up to the agitated mob and, in a second, cut the towrope, tumbling the mobsters over one another and saving the machine.

There were other sources of opposition against Porter and the steamer. Porter recalled that hardly a day passed during the first year the engine was in service that someone didn't come into the engine house and "shoot his mouth off" against the folly of maintaining so expensive an institution and especially railing against the inequity of "paying him seventy-five dollars a month to loaf around the house and do nothing."

One man came in so often that Porter began to look for him about once a week. For a long time, the engineer didn't know the man's name, but he later learned that the offender was Mr. Charles Baker, a leading democrat in the city.

In March 1860, five months after the Machigonne was commissioned, Baker was appointed City Marshal, a position now commonly known as chief of police. Porter related to a Portland newspaper in 1896 that Marshal Baker came into the engine house even more frequently, always railing against Porter and the steam fire engine. In April 1860, the department turned out for a fire at the Chestnut Street Church. Machigonne No. 1 was located at a reservoir pumping into hose lines to the fire. Heavy fire from the church extended to the cornice of the adjacent building—City Hall. Marshal Baker reported the fire to the chief engineer, Samuel Leavitt, who ordered the hand fire engines to direct their hose lines to the cornice, but the streams fell short. A line from the steamer was swung around, sweeping the cornice and eaves of the huge building and knocking the fire down quickly.

Brands from the burning church were also landing on houses on Cumberland Street, which were themselves becoming involved. Upon receiving word of these fires, Marshal Baker ran to report the Cumberland Street fires to the foreman of the Machigonne. The firemen ran a line down the block and successfully extinguished the fires. Later in the night, during the church fire, a crowd, becoming boisterous, gathered around the steamer.

Engine house of Machigonne No. 1, former quarters of Casco Hand Fire Engine No. 1, since 1854. Extant. *Courtesy of Portland Fire Museum Collection.*

The crowd members were shouting against Porter and the engine when Marshal Baker broke through the crowd and loudly asked Porter if he could use more room to operate his engine. Porter answered, "A little more room wouldn't hurt."

Baker ordered four of his police patrolmen to move the mob off Chestnut Street. Baker was now convinced of the value of the steam fire engine and its engineer, Edward W. Porter.

The source of water for fighting fire was fifty-nine reservoirs and ten wells. These were filled by rain and often did not hold sufficient water. The hand engines soon exhausted the supply and were forced to move to other reservoirs during a fire. The steam fire engine emptied a reservoir in less than fifteen minutes.

A movement was made by citizen groups in the early 1860s, led by Mr. Francis Ormond Jonathan Smith, to construct a water system to supply water for fighting fire and for domestic use. Smith offered to fund the construction as a private enterprise. The plan was to charge rates equivalent to those of Boston. Following extensive meetings, discussions and estimates, Smith failed to convince the officials at City Hall to legally authorize the vital water project. According to the *Portland Daily Advertiser*, the massive undertaking was obstructed by Portland officials.

As a consequence, the fire department was obliged to maintain and rely on the inadequate reservoirs, which were certain to freeze in the winter and likely to evaporate in the summer, and the twelve wells.

A second steam fire engine, Falmouth No. 2, with a pumping capacity of six hundred gallons per minute, was placed in service in March 1861.

This piece was built at the Portland Company works on Fore Street. The Portland Company was nationally known for its more than six hundred high-quality steam railroad locomotives and numerous Johnson steam fire engines. This pumper tested satisfactorily, and the *Portland Daily Advertiser* wrote:

> *The Falmouth is a very neat and tasteful machine, devoid of extra embellishment, and intended for service rather than show. She is of the first class, and weighs something more than 6000 pounds.*

The Falmouth No. 2 was housed at Congress Street at the head of Smith Street. With the addition of this new steam fire engine, another hand engine company was sure to be decommissioned. The official word was received the following June. The *Eastern Argus* of June 14, 1861, reported:

Falmouth Steam Fire Engine No. 2, built by the Portland Company in this city in 1861 and located in the Congress Street Engine House, at the head of Smith Street. *Courtesy of Portland Fire Museum Collection.*

The Portland Board of Aldermen, Standing Committee on the Fire Department, reported that in consultation with the Board of Engineers, they had come to the conclusion that the services of one of the companies could be dispensed with without impairing the efficiency of the Department, and the Board of Engineers unanimously designated Tiger Engine Co. No. 3 as the one that should be disbanded. An order was therefore passed, honorably discharging the officers and members of that company from service in the Fire Department, from and after the first day of July next.

On March 19, 1861, the *Portland Daily Advertiser* noted:

Order to sell the three fire engines taken from the disbanded companies, the proceeds to be applied to meet deficiencies in the appropriations in the Fire Department, was passed in concurrence.

The chief engineer, in his 1861 report, extended his sentiments:

It gives me pleasure to add my testimony to that so often expressed by my fellow citizens and the press, for the promptness with which the members of the Department respond when their services are needed, ready at all times to sacrifice ease and health for the public good. Many of those connected with this Department at the commencement of this year, have not only made the above sacrifices, but that of homes and friends dear to them—not to fight an enemy of our neighborhood, or village, or city, but an enemy to and destroyer of this blessed Union. May they be as successful abroad as have their brethren at home.

As a matter of statistics, the Portland Fire Department responded to 382 alarms from 1849 to 1859. From 1860 to 1865, 196 alarms were answered.

Even with the Fire Alarm District system established in 1858, the alarm was often inaccurate and deceiving, according to a *Portland Sunday Press and Times* article. A lifelong resident recalled that the method was to yell "Fire!" as loud as possible. The fire was usually in the stage of a column of smoke and fire. People were apt to run toward a sound when they are looking for excitement. If a man standing at Congress Street and Preble Street should hear another man shouting "Fire!" down on Portland Street, he would naturally lift up his own voice and start on the run. If men on Center Street heard the shout, they might run for the waterfront, in the opposite direction, thinking the shout came from that direction. The shouting was picked up and continued all across the city streets. Police were provided with keys to the churches; the tolling of the bells added to the confusion. If a man heard the First Parish Church bell, he would run there, when actually the fire was distant.

Samuel F.B. Morse transmitted his message—"What hath God wrought?"—over a telegraph line from Baltimore to Washington on May 24, 1844. This major step in communication was an object of great interest to two fire enthusiasts. Dr. William Channing of Boston and Mr. Moses Farmer of Salem set about designing an electric system for giving the alarm of fire by adopting the principals of Morse's telegraph.

In June 1845, Dr. Channing wrote of a plan he conceived for the use of the electric telegraph as a means of giving the alarm of fire, which would be received at a central office. The alarm would then be transmitted in the same manner. In 1847, Farmer, a telegraph operator and engineer, began working with Dr. Channing devising a fire alarm box. It was cast iron, sixteen inches high, eleven inches wide and four inches deep, with the shape of a gabled house. A door to the box was equipped with a substantial spring lock with two levers. The workings inside the box consisted of a board supporting a lighting arrester, a magnet and armature, a crank and toothed wheel and a spring key. The spring key and crank were used to open and close the signal circuits to send the alarm to the office. The toothed wheel had projections that, by operating on the circuit, gave two groups of symbols on the register and the office bells, showing the number of the district and station from which the alarm had come.

In 1848, Boston mayor Josiah Quincy became interested enough to look into the matter. A demonstration was set up for the mayor and the public. Two machines for striking church bells were struck by telegraph from New York City, proving the feasibility of Dr. Channing's claims. In spite of a successful demonstration, the matter rested until 1851, when action was finally taken. The Boston City Council appointed a Joint Special Committee on June 16, 1851, to carry out the construction of a telegraphic fire alarm system. Dr. William Channing was named superintendent of construction.

Their achievement was rewarded when, in 1852, on April 28, the Boston Fire Alarm Telegraph was placed in commission with thirty-nine "stations," or fire alarm boxes. This was the first electric fire alarm telegraph system in the world.

Interest in such an alarm system was mounting in Portland among the firemen and officers who had been reading of the alarm system in newspapers and trade publications.

On March 11, 1861, Portland Fire Department chief engineer Harris Barnes was ordered by the board of aldermen "to investigate the working of the Fire Alarm Telegraph system in cities where it is used and place such facts in regard to its efficiency as may be likely to be of public interest and benefit in his annual Report."

Chief Barnes boarded a train to spend a day inspecting the fire alarm telegraph system in Boston. The fire alarm office was located in the City Building at 21 Court Street in downtown Boston. The office of the Boston chief engineer was in the same building.

Upon his return to Portland, Chief Barnes wrote his report to the board of aldermen. The report, with the writer's observations, follows:

In compliance with this Order I visited Boston, where I had reason to believe the system was in perfect operation, that city having been the first in the United States to adopt it. By the kind attentions of the Superintendent of the Fire Telegraph, and the Chief Engineer of the Fire Department of Boston, I was enabled to examine the system thoroughly and in its minutest details.

The Boston Telegraph provides for forty eight signal boxes scattered over the city, from any one of which a definite alarm of fire can be sent instantaneously into the Central station, connected with the Chief Engineer's department, by merely turning a crank. It connects also twenty three alarm bells, in all parts of the city, with the Central station, so they can be struck the District number of the fire by the touch of one man's finger at the centre. It also enables the Superintendent, or Operator, at the Central station, during an alarm of fire, to tap back, on all the signal boxes, the number of the signal box in the District from which the alarm of fire first came. The following results are obtained by this arrangement.

In this opening statement, Chief Barnes writes a clear overview, describing the operation of the fire alarm telegraph system in Boston, following his tour conducted by Boston chief engineer George W. Bird and superintendent of fire alarm Joseph B. Stearns. Chief Barnes emphasizes how efficient and well designed the system is.

1ˢᵗ The alarms of fire are brought under control of the Central Station, connected with the Department. As a practical result of the system, false alarms have almost ceased.

Word-of-mouth alarms and the sextants being located to ring the church bells cost valuable time. The fire department, at times, turned out for the ringing of bells for other reasons. The result: a false alarm.

2ⁿᵈ An alarm of fire is communicated from any part of the city instantaneously to the Centre, and from thence is instantaneously struck by telegraph on all the bells. An average saving of from fifteen to twenty minutes, in getting the alarm to all the engines, is probably thus obtained over the old system of ringing each bell by hand.

The instantaneous and regular striking of bells was clearer and better defined than a jumble in the air of five church bells.

3ʳᵈ The engines are concentrated, not only upon the District, but upon the very signal box nearest the fire, from which the alarm first proceeded, so that no distance is lost in running to the fire.

Districts were large, and it was difficult to locate the fire. Time was often lost on the run. The comparisons that Chief Barnes makes apply to Portland, which used the same church bell system that Boston abandoned in 1852.

4th Although so many bells are used, greater regularity and certainty exist in striking the alarm than the old system, where a bell ringer was required to each bell. With a few large bells, the application of the system would be still more simple.

Box numbers struck simultaneously over bells simplified and enabled better communications and responses.

5th From all these reasons, the effect of the system is to diminish losses by fire, and especially the danger of great conflagrations.

Chief Barnes seemed to be a prophet with the words "great conflagrations," yet firemen were mindful and constantly on guard against all disasters. At this juncture in the report, each of the five points were substantial, especially the comparison of Boston's successful telegraph system with the former hand ringing and district system still in use in Portland. Barnes's report is firm and convincing: "This brief summery of its workings, I gather from Mr. Stearns, the Superintendent of the Fire Alarm Telegraph, and my own observation."

At this point in his report, the narrative takes a sudden turn. This leads us to the conclusion that upon the chief's enthusiastic report, something caused him to recommend against the purchase of a fire alarm telegraph system. Was he influenced by political pressure not to recommend a system such as this because of cost? Was it too large a project for him to oversee? The chief engineer was a part-time, annually elected official.

The reasons that the chief sites at this point are weak at best, especially when compared to the strength of his observations and conclusions about the Boston system:

The system works admirably in great cities like Boston and New York, where the population is spread over a large surface of territory. But in a city the size of Portland, under our present arrangement of Fire Alarms, and with an efficient night Police, the introduction of the Fire Telegraph would be of but little service. I am very sure its advantages would not be commensurate with the expense of putting it into operation and working it.

This closing paragraph was not written with the same positive attitude as the first part of the report. When Boston installed the fire alarm telegraph in 1852, the city was not much larger in "surface territory" than Portland in 1861.

In his report, Barnes cites results, which he has numbered 1, 2, 3 and 4, that underscore the superiority of the fire telegraph over the manual ringing of the church bells "and with the efficient night police." The police, discovering a fire, still had to raise the shout of "Fire!" and locate five sextons to ring the church bell to sound the alarm.

This line "The introduction of the Fire Telegraph would be of but little service" plainly contradicts the foregoing major part of his report: "I am very sure its advantages would not be commensurate with the expense."

Chief Barnes made the following points in his report to the aldermen about alarms controlled by a central office: fifteen to twenty minutes of time could be saved in response by the instantaneous striking of alarms, engines responding to the box location and the regularity of the bell striking, the effect being to diminish losses by fire, especially the danger of great conflagrations. Within five years, Portland would suffer the greatest loss in America by conflagration to that date. Contributing factors included delayed alarm and response time.

Portland was, at that time, a principal city in New England and America. It was a terminus for the St. Lawrence and Atlantic Railroad. Midwest grain was shipped to Portland by rail through the St. Lawrence and Atlantic line. Each year, the St. Lawrence River froze, preventing all shipping and increasing the dependence on the railroad. Portland was the closest port to Montreal, and the extensive Grand Trunk Railroad yards were busy. Enormous wharves were serviced by nine tracks with large sheds, huge enclosed conveyers, stockyards, a passenger station and a large roundhouse. The Kennebec and Portland Railroad and York and Cumberland Railroad ran tracks and trains to freight sheds and passenger depots in different parts of the city. Seagoing steamboats made regularly scheduled trips from Portland to Boston and New York, as well as transatlantic voyages.

On Fore Street, the waterfront, the Portland Company built more than six hundred steam locomotive engines for the American railroads and other heavy railroad equipment. The J.B. Johnson patent steam fire engine was a brand manufactured by the Portland Company.

An eight-story brick factory building near Commercial and Maple Streets produced sugar made from West Indies molasses through a steam process developed by Portland's John B. Brown.

The waterfront was enlarged in 1852 with the construction of Commercial Street, entirely made of fill. One hundred feet wide at its narrowest point and a mile long, it was lined with huge brick and granite warehouses fed by multiple tracks to the loading docks or entering the buildings. Assorted tracks ran down the center of the street, with numerous side tracks connecting the twenty-seven wharves extending into the Fore River.

On Middle Street, the heart of the business and financial district, four- and five-story brick buildings and large ornate hotels lined the street. Most of the buildings in this section of the city were red brick with slate or composite roofs. They were well kept, with painted trim and appealing signs and store windows. Horse-drawn wagons, carriages and pushcarts filled the streets. Thousands of single- and multiple-family homes, most of wood frame, stood in the crowded neighborhoods of Oxford, Washington, Cumberland and Franklin Streets.

This is the Portland that had no continuous water supply, the Portland that had no fire alarm telegraph system, the Portland that had decommissioned nine fire engine companies and discharged 406 firemen.

With the purchase of the third steam fire engine with a pumping capacity of seven hundred gallons per minute and the organization of Steam Fire Engine Company Cumberland No. 3 on September 16, 1862, Hand Fire Engine Company Portland No. 5 was ordered decommissioned.

Cumberland Steam Fire Engine No. 3, an Amoskeag engine built in 1862. The engine was relocated to the Brackett Street firehouse in the West End in 1864. *Courtesy of Portland Fire Museum Collection.*

Cumberland Steam Fire Engine Company No. 3 was placed in a brick firehouse at 176 Bracket Street, near Bradford Street.

The 1802 Bramah antique hand engine Cataract No. 2 had been out of service for eighteen years. The city council ordered, on March 3, 1863, that the "old lobster" be permanently displayed in a passageway in the basement of the new, grand, ornate City Hall.

Casco Steam Fire Engine No. 5, a Portland Company Engine, went into service in early 1864 at Congress, at the head of Smith Street, and then relocated to Congress near Lime Street with Ladder No. 1. *Courtesy of Portland Fire Museum Collection.*

A new steam engine was placed in service in 1864, designated Casco No. 5. This pumper was built by the Portland Company on Fore Street and was a second-class pumper, meaning it was capable of pumping four hundred gallons per minute. The steamer weighed sixty-two hundred pounds and was located on Congress Street at the head of Smith Street. At this time, the steamer Falmouth No. 2, which was experiencing many mechanical problems, was placed in reserve.[17]

In July 1864, the company clerk wrote in the company log of Falmouth Steam Fire Engine Company No. 2:

> *Regular monthly meeting of Falmouth Engine Co No 2. Captain Russell in the chair. Meeting called to order at 7 ½ o'clock—Record of last meeting read and approved. Captain Russell then notified the company that they had been disbanded by the City, not having any steamer for the Company, the Falmouth having "Played out" and they had concluded not to repair her at present, but to purchase a new steamer.*

Portland Steam Fire Engine No. 2, a Portland Company Engine, went into service in early 1865 and was quartered in the new Munjoy Hill firehouse on Congress Street at the head of North Street. *Courtesy of Portland Fire Museum Collection.*

On motion voted to petition the City for the new steamer. After the customary thanks to the officers—adjourned.

Wm. P Horrie Clerk

Another four-hundred-gallon-per-minute steam fire engine, built by the Portland Company, which was filling orders for steam fire engines for fire departments across the United States, was placed in service with a newly organized crew on January 6, 1865. The company was named Portland Steam Fire Engine Company No. 2 and was quartered on Congress Street at the head of North Street on Munjoy Hill.

RECOMMENDATIONS
AND REJECTIONS

The steam engine Falmouth was repaired and designated a reserve engine company. It was located in the house on Congress Street at the head of Smith Street. Casco No. 5 was then relocated to the house on Congress at Lime Street.

In 1865, the chief engineer officially requested the replacement of the hand-drawn truck that Washington Hook & Ladder No. 1 was running:

> *Hook & Ladder carriage No. 1, which is the only carriage having a company attached it, and upon which our chief reliance is placed in case of fire, having seen much service, is consequently much out of repair; and I would recommend to your honorable body the purchase of a new one with all the modern improvements.*

This truck had been in service since 1840 and carried four ladders, four hooks for pulling down buildings, nine axes and lengths of rope, chains and other equipment. There were two spare ladder carriages, one built in 1827 and the other built in 1835. Each of these ladder trucks, or carriages, was old and worn out. The chief was requesting a replacement, a heavier, hand-drawn truck carrying 172 feet of ladders and nine hooks.

He also noted that the City of Roxbury, Massachusetts, now had three steam fire engines with one pair of horses provided for each exclusively, thereby rendering the fire department more effective and efficient. This was important due to the fact that the Portland Fire Department owned no horses, although four steamers and a ladder truck were being run.

The chief also reported the purchase of two thousand feet of the first quality leading hose suitable for the use of steamers. Each of the four hose carriages carried one thousand feet of leading hose.

This comparison to Roxbury was also made by noted writer John Neal:[18]

> *The Fire Department—*[is] *not what it should be. It must be enlarged and reformed. Our average yearly loss by fire from 1843–1849 was $103,795. Both inclusive. From 1854–1859 $46,867.84. From 1860–1865 $42,305. Yet we have only four steamers, with fifteen men each, one Hook and Ladder with twenty men, and five men constituting the Board of Engineers—in all but eighty-five men.*

The fire department average annual expenditure, according to Neal, was $11,000.00. By contrast, Roxbury had a population of thirty thousand with an annual expenditure of no less than $27,522.11 on the fire department. Roxbury was near or bordered Boston, Charlestown, Chelsea and Cambridge, while Portland was fourteen miles from the nearest help. Neal noted that the Roxbury average yearly loss over fourteen years was $18,900.00. A city of comparable population that provided greater funding resulted in lower fire losses.

Neal's point regarding the surrounding cities being able to supply mutual aid in a minimal amount of time is a serious one. Actually, the Portland fire loss from 1854 to 1859 amounted to $211,297, and from 1860 to 1865, it was $206,421.

Portland Steam Fire Engine Company No. 2 was organized in 1865, resulting in the decommissioning of Hand Fire Engine Companies Torrent No. 6 and Ocean No. 4 and Pacific Hand Fire Engine Company No. 9. At this point, the elimination of the eight hand engine companies resulted in the reduction of more than 480 firemen.

The city auditor's report of March 1866 stated:

> *Fire Department—The expenditures in this department, including pay to companies and engineers of steam fire engine, have been $13,620.37, being a decrease from the previous year of $8,143.02. The department now consists of four steamers in full commission, one hook and ladder company, and one steamer held in reserve, ready for use in cases of emergency. Two*

hand engines have disbanded during the year, which, however, only accounts in part for the decrease of expenditure this year as compared with former years, a saving having been made in the ordinary expenses this year over those of last year of $7,771.32. This favorable result is largely due to the fact that there was a less number of severe fires than usual, and the department was relieved from the necessity of purchasing any new hose during the year.

In the same annual report, the chief engineer wrote:

I recommend to your honorable body, the purchase of two thousand feet of first quality leading hose, suitable for the use of steamers. I recommend to the next City Council the construction of a first class reservoir on Lincoln or Oxford Streets, or in that vicinity, as there has been more wooden buildings erected in this section the past few years than any other portion of the city, and consequently we should be compelled to use the water from the back bay in case of fire, and than only at high tide. There is not a reservoir on Lincoln Street, nor Oxford Street below Pearl Street to Washington Street, and in my judgment, that part of the city is more exposed to an extensive conflagration should a fire occur at a time when the water was out of the back bay.

The log of an engine company recorded, "April 4, 1866—Wet[19] machine at the corner of State and Pine Streets. Worked about a half an hour Burst hose and went home. Machine worked to satisfaction of all present."

The focus of the fire officers and firefighters in their reports was on the limited water supply and the failing condition of the hose.

On April 28, 1866, at one o'clock in the morning, the companies responded to a large fire in a brick stable on Temple Street. Five horses and a number of sleighs and carriages were lost in the fire. The department operated for four hours, during which time Steam Fire Engine Company Casco No. 5 was severely damaged while pumping. The pumper in reserve, Falmouth No. 4, now thoroughly overhauled and repaired, was assigned to Casco No. 5 as decisions were made regarding the repair of that company's disabled pumper. There were still no horses assigned to the fire department exclusively for the purpose of drawing apparatus. The plan was, upon the alarm of fire, to locate the street department horse team, or teams, or privately owned horses and bring them to the nearest firehouse, connect

them to the apparatus and begin the run. In March 1866, Chief Engineer
Ezra Russell wrote:

> *I recommend to the next City Council the purchase of another pair of
> horses, and that all the steam fire engines be hauled to and from the fire
> by horses belonging to the city; As it is, and has been the case, that on an
> alarm of fire in the day time, the horses have been invariably employed at
> least a mile from the engine to which they were attached, and where their
> services were needed, and I trust your honorable board will see at a glance
> the absolute necessity of having at least one pair of horses at all times ready
> harnessed at one of the central engine houses of one of our steamers.*
>
> *I will state a case: At the late fire on Canal, foot of State Street, at the
> P.S. & P.R.R. Depot, the horses that were attached to the steamer located
> on Congress Street opposite North Street, were busily employed near State
> Street, and consequently considerable time must necessarily elapse before the
> steamer* [the Portland] *could be brought to the fire. In the intervening time,
> the fire had made such progress that before subdued, the loss incident to our
> delay, was some thousands of dollars. As it was, the steamer Cumberland,
> kept on Brackett Street, was the first to put a stream of water upon the
> fire, and the horses that were used for this steamer at this time, were also
> at work at or near the Grand Trunk Depot. One of the steamers belonging
> to this department is now hauled to and from fires by horses hired for this
> purpose, at a cost of four hundred dollars per annum—making at the rate
> of sixteen dollars per fire for the past year—the Department having been
> called out twenty five times. I would respectfully suggest that one pair of
> the city horses be kept at one of the central engine houses during each day,
> and changed alternately. The pair which I have recommended the purchase
> of, including the three pair now in use, could, in my opinion, be made
> decidedly advantageous to the Fire Department, and at the same time meet
> the approbation of all our citizens who feel at heart the welfare and interest
> of the city. The city of Roxbury, Mass., have now in use three steam fire
> engines, and one pair of horses are provided for each engine exclusively,
> thereby rendering their Department more effective and efficient.*

The steam fire engines were successful in the battle on Middle Street on
June 16 at the five-story brick mill of the Cory Furniture Company—heavy
fire in a building in a district that was densely compact. The fire companies,
four steamers and a ladder company, operated for five hours and held the fire

in the building of origin, saving a section and its contents from fire damage. The spring had brought so little rain that the reservoirs used at this fire were nearly emptied.

Chief Rogers wrote in his log:

> *Fire discovered Saturday evening at 7:35 o'clock at Cory Furniture Manufacturing on Middle Street between Plum Street and Exchange Street—Second floor near the elevator—fire in shaft, up and down, all five floors, quickly extinguished—attic lumber in storage—roof burned off—lines into the fire from adjacent buildings. Worked six hours—four steamers worked beautifully.*

The firemen, their officers and their apparatus were accomplishing their goal of battling major fires in the city and, furthermore, keeping the fires from extending. The fire companies proved, repeatedly, that they had the ability to handle a major fire under the worst conditions.

An entry in the log of Steam Fire Engine Co. Cumberland No. 3:

> *An alarm of fire was given by the burning of the brick stable of Henry Taylor and Co.—situated on Temple Street. The engine was taken to the reservoir in Market Square and got second water upon the fire. Played about five hours. The engine worked splendidly considering the POOR hose in use.*

The Temple Street fire and the Middle Street fire, as well as many other serious building fires, affirm that the Portland Fire Department was capable of attacking fire and cutting it off, thereby saving valuable property, in spite of old leather and hemp hoses that were inadequate for service.

However, the reduction in apparatus and firemen was undoubtedly being felt at each serious fire. Where there had been 417 firemen, there were now 140.

The department was in a state of conversion, with a change in personnel, apparatus and leadership. The nine hand fire engines, with their fifty- to sixty-man rosters and their individual brightly colored uniforms and social gatherings, were now eliminated by smoke-belching steam pumpers, drawn by horses, which required crews of only fifteen men. Many of the firemen who had been chasing fires with the hand tubs since the 1840s saw the steam age eliminating them, as well. At this time, it was a scene being repeated throughout the Northeast. Old-time firefighters did not see the steam pumpers as wonderful inventions that made fighting fire faster and more efficient.

The hand fire engine men understandably resisted steam fire engines. They were being replaced by paid full-time men, whereas they had been paid only per alarm. The fire company had been their social lives, their political lives and part of their business lives. They had achieved certain notoriety and an active interest in the protection of human life, property and commerce. The occupations of these firemen ranged from house painters to lawyers and from bankers to teamsters. They were elected into the companies for the sheer pleasure of pulling the heavy fire engines, some weighing one ton or more, through the rain, ice and four feet of snow. They pumped to exhaustion and were fined for missing an alarm or company meeting. Election to some sort of beautification committee would have been less taxing, but these good citizens held a true commitment to the well being of Portland exhibited by few, then or now.

Many viewed the changes as a disassembling of the established fire department, and they were waiting for the fire that the steamers would not be able to handle, one where they could wag their heads and say, "I told you so."

FIRE!

Portland was celebrating ninety years of independence from British rule, a victory in which their Falmouth Neck predecessors had played an important role. Since the end of the Civil War, this was the first opportunity for celebration. Some of the planned festivities included a traveling circus with a hippopotamus and trained dancing elephants, a balloon inflation and ascension at noon in Deering's pasture and a huge parade and brass bands. A military muster with fifes and drums and performances around town built the excitement in preparation for the most brilliant display of fireworks in the evening.

A lad on Commercial Street at the corner of Maple Street lit a celebratory firecracker. He tossed it into a pile of wood shavings in Deguio's boatyard, which was filled with the supplies and lumber to construct boats. The yard was not neat and tidy; in fact, throughout the city, especially at the waterfront and in many other industrial areas, good housekeeping was not enforced and was rarely observed. Piles of lumber, scraps, sawdust and shavings were common, not only at Deguio's boat shop, but also everywhere. The shavings easily ignited, and the harbor wind propelled the tiny fire, quickly igniting a wooden boat shed.

With almost no appreciable rainfall for months, and day after day of high temperatures, the summer sun was baking the dirt streets, roofs, reservoirs, lumber, trees, buildings and outside storage. Everything was dry. William W. Ruby,[20] in the vicinity on Commercial Street, spotted the fire, which was now extending into the wood-frame boat shop, a building that has been described as being able to be carried off by a dozen men. He started the hearty shout of "Fire! Fire! Maple Street! District Eight!" as the heat and fire extended to a larger, two-and-a-half-story wood-frame building and then rolled on to involve an eight-story brick sugar factory.

Steam Fire Engine Company Cumberland No. 3 wrote in its log:

> *An alarm of fire was given about five o'clock in the afternoon caused by the burning of Deguio's Boat Shop situated on Commercial Street. The Engine was promptly on hand and got first water before the fire, which soon spread to the adjoining Buildings with great rapidity. The machine was soon ordered to the Reservoir on the corner of Danforth and Maple Streets and the fire was prevented from crossing Danforth Street, by so doing.[21] The members were all present and worked beautifully, but the fire swept along Fore Street to Cotton and Centre Streets, and so on, across the City from the Boat Shop on Commercial Street to private dwellings on South Street,*

The John B. Brown sugar refinery building was destroyed early in the conflagration. *Courtesy of Maine Historical Society.*

Fire!

burning nearly all principal Buildings in Town, and sweeping over nearly nine miles of Streets and about three hundred and thirty Acres of the City.

Granville H. Cloyes, Clerk

Alfred Wiggin, the engineer of Steam Fire Engine Cumberland No. 3, provided the following narrative on the thirtieth anniversary of the conflagration. One of the veterans of the Portland Fire Department, Wiggin helped to fight the flames, on duty for twenty-five hours. His steamer, Cumberland No. 3, rattled down Maple Street just behind Machigonne to take water from the docks. As they went down the street, the fire had already become so hot that Wiggin had to pull his hat down over his face to keep it from burning.

We were going so fast that if anything had gone wrong we should be all piled up, but it was so hot, that we could not go any other way. The Cumberland did not stay long on the lower side of the fire. Like Machigonne, she made a circuit and did gallant service on Danforth Street where she threw water onto a house on the corner of Maple Street and saved it, probably keeping the fire from leaping the street. Cumberland pumped dry the reservoir on the corner of Maple and Danforth streets and was then moved up to a court to an old cellar which was full of water. Had the fire covered Danforth Street, the engine would have never come out of the court. Later, the Cumberland was stationed in front of the First Parish Church and then she was moved diagonally across the city to the dump, stopping at the water supplies on the way and here and there, saving a house which would otherwise have been burned.

Some confusion at the sounding of the fire alarm on the church bells was caused when reports circulated through the streets of the city about the location of the fire. One eyewitness recalled:

All sorts of stories were abroad. The fire was located in half dozen places, and more than once, the cry of "All Out!" was heard and the alarm bells stopped for a season, only to be set a going again with more vehemence than ever.

This confusion on the part of the citizenry was understandable, as was the delay in the alarm.

At the corner of Cumberland and Franklin Streets, the engine stayed until the heat broke the glass in the ornamental lantern behind the driver's seat. Wiggin continued, "When that heavy glass was splintered, I thought it was time to get out of that place and we hitched up. While the horses were being put in, we had to brush the sparks off their backs." This report does not seem to demonstrate a fire department with no training, discipline or plan.

The natural wind, as reported, blowing a gale and the updrafts of the conflagration took burned papers and articles as far away as New Meadows, approximately thirty miles away. A burning fragment of wood was blown to the east, dropping on the roof of a Munjoy Hill house. In minutes, that house and two more were involved in heavy fire and destroyed.

Out at sea, Captain G.M. Dinsmore, on the schooner *Clara*, sighted the glow from the conflagration from Jonesport, 124 sea miles away.

Wagons being driven through the Portland streets, piled high with furniture and belongings to be taken to a safe place, were set ablaze from

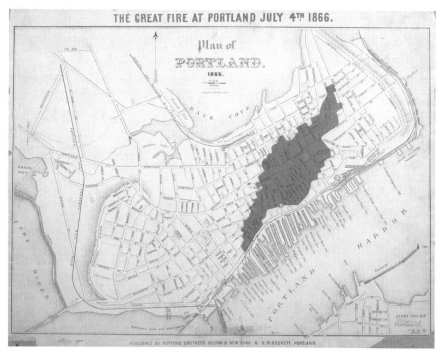

Map of the conflagration's burnt area of city. *Courtesy of Maine Historical Society.*

burning brands. The drivers were completely unaware of the fire at their backs. According to John Neal, a merchant on India Street,

near the foot of Middle Street, finding he had no time to lose, began to remove the merchandise from his shop, by lugging off a large box of tobacco, which he left, as he believed, in a place of safety. On returning to the shop, he found it on fire, with little chance of saving any thing more. Seizing a quantity of provisions, he started for the wharf, where his family had betaken themselves for safety, and met a stranger carrying off the very box of tobacco he had so carefully saved. The thief was hailed; he made no answer, but quickened his pace, and the trader, dropped his provisions, gave chase. On overtaking the fellow, he gave him two or three blows, and tumbled him into the gutter. Then, after having secured his tobacco a second time, and again depositing it in a safe place, he went back for the provisions he had dropped on the way. Having made sure of all he could find, he hurried back to the spot where he left the tobacco—it was no longer there—it had wholly disappeared.

GREAT DESIDERATUM: WATER

Steam Fire Engine Company Portland No. 2 recorded in its log:

The alarm this afternoon was caused by fire being discovered in Deguio's Boat Shop on Commercial Street. The Department were promptly on the Ground, but owing to the high wind, the fire soon communicated to the planning mill and Brown's Sugar House, and from there, spread in a North-Easterly direction across the City. Burning everything in it's course.

The following is from the handwritten log of Portland Engine No. 2:

Our Engine was first stationed on Brown's Wharf where we had just got a stream on the fire when we were ordered to Union Street, it being reported to the Chief Engineer that Bond & Merrill Shop was on fire. After getting our Engine in position, we soon found that there was no fire in the Building and we were ordered on Fore Street to foot of Center Street, where we put 2 streams on to the fire, soon exhausting the reservoir.

We were next stationed on Free Street, corner of Center Street, after playing[22] the reservoir dry, we next shifted to Market Square with Line down Center Street, where we effectively put a stop to the further progress of the fire in that direction.[23] We again shifted to Cumberland, at corner of Chestnut Street, with the line on Congress Street, enjoyed in wetting down Buildings around the City Hall, the water soon played out.

We again shifted to Cedar Street, and while we were trying to find hose, the fire burst out on the Dome of City hall. We again shifted to Congress Street, playing out of the Cistern in the basement of the Hall, with the line inside the building, playing directly on to the fire, staying in there as long as it was safe for us, as we could not make any headway against the fire. We again shifted to Cedar Street, with pipe[24] on Chestnut Street wetting down Buildings in the rear of the Hall. After danger had passed in that direction, we again shifted to City hall and played on the Ruins. We next went to Market Square and Played on the Heaton Building as long as we could find water to play, after which, we returned to the House, having been on the ground for 17 hours, constantly at work, without any help. Reel filled Roll Call Omitted.

Thomas Dame, Clerk

Machigonne Engine Company No. 1 responded and worked at first on the waterfront and ended operations at the United States Hotel in Market Square at eleven o'clock at night on July 6, two days after the fire started. The pumper was forced to move in the search of water eight times, exhausting the water supply frequently. The hoses were burned off the pumper three times.

The log of Chief Engineer Spencer Rodgers reported on Steam Fire Engine Casco No. 5:

Disabled at the Temple Street fire on April 28th, and which after being examined, was condemned, and stored in the Engine House on Congress Street near the head of India Street, and finally destroyed at the great fire on July 4th.

At this time, the amount of leather leading hose on the hose reels amounted to 9,400 feet. Hemp leading hose was 550 feet. This may appear to be a substantial amount, but it was below standard, especially when compared to the length of the streets and building frontage burned in the conflagration, which, if laid end to end, was fourteen miles long.

Fire!

The Congress Street Engine House at the head of Smith Street was destroyed in the conflagration, along with Casco No. 5, which was stored inside the building. *Courtesy of Portland Fire Museum Collection.*

The log of Washington Hook and Ladder Company No. 1 reported:

Company called out to a fire about 4 o'clock PM, which commenced on Commercial Street and burned across the City to Munjoy Hill destroying Fifteen-Million Dollars worth of Property. Returned to House in about three days, no Roll was called, as it was thought by the First Director that every man had done all he could.

Albert G. Corliss, Clerk.

A certain amount of these records are repetitive; however, each is presented here unedited because the reports plainly show the tactics employed by the fire companies and the limitations within which the men had to work.

At this point, it becomes clear that historians and writers have long misrepresented the facts of the actions of the Portland Fire Department regarding the conflagration of 1866. The writer who said that "the fire started on the Portland waterfront while city firefighters were enjoying a holiday picnic at Sebago Lake" conducted no fact checking. The records clearly show that "the Department was promptly on the Ground." That same writer proclaimed in 2008, "Hoses weren't long enough to stretch to where the fire was burning." This is demonstrated to be untrue by Portland No. 2, the "Engine first stationed on Brown's Wharf where we had just got a stream on the fire."

As the logs show, the historian, repeating the Portland transcript report, was inaccurate when he said:

> *Portland was greatly hampered by her fire department in trying to stop the conflagration. The department was an ill trained volunteer staff. At the start of the fire many companies and their equipment were attending the celebration; They were not ready for an emergency.*

The clerks record the actions of their companies. The logs were subject to scrutiny by chief engineers and insurance companies and as such they were expected to be correct. The above logs agree on the basic fundamentals of the fire and the actions of the fire department.

A historian putting forth that the fire department was ill trained does not recognize the fact that the members of the steam fire engine companies responded immediately and upon arrival lost no time in setting up the pumper and laying out the leather two-and-a-half-inch hose. They located water sources and played their hose lines on the fire.

Operating a steam fire engine's pumps requires extensive training. One must stoke the boiler, draw a draft to pump the water and maintain the proper pump pressure for a long hose line of approximately four hundred feet. It takes training to stretch and operate the hose line in proximity to the fire. As already determined, the men and apparatus were not attending to anything but the control of this fire, and they did so with skill.

"They were not ready for an emergency." These companies responded to the emergency. They were faced with a strong wind from the harbor, a lack of water, a densely built city and reduced manpower.

The records show that the statements "Flames soon engulfed the building and spread to an adjoining one. Firemen easily extinguished the blaze and left." were absurd. Companies worked for seventeen hours without a break.

One of the tactics employed by the engine companies was to attack the fire from the perimeter of the conflagration. Portland Steam Fire Engine Company No. 2 reported, "We next shifted to Market Square with line down Center Street where we effectively put a stop to further progress of the fire in that direction."

Fire!

Oil painting of the Second Parish Church on Middle Street during the conflagration. *Attributed to Woodbury Hatch, member of Volunteer Hand Fire Engine Company No. 3. Collection of Maine Historical Society.*

Cumberland Steam Fire Engine No. 3 noted, "The machine was soon ordered to Reservoir on corner of Danforth and Maple Streets and the fire was prevented from crossing Danforth Street by doing so."

The fire had gained conflagration force by this time, but it was defiantly not going with "no check anywhere." Reservoirs did not contain capacity water due to previous fires and a lack of rainfall.

The conflagration map shows the jagged edges of the red area. This shows the engine companies cutting the fire off, then locating another water source and cutting it off again a block away. Some companies leapfrogged continually a block or two to gain control of the perimeter of the conflagration, pumping all available water. This tactic was effective, and no ill-trained fire department could have been so successful.

The log of the chief engineer of the Portland Fire Department gave the following report:

Fire was discovered this afternoon at ¼ to 5 in the Boat Shop of J.C. Deguio on Commercial Street near the corner of Maple Street, which proved to be the most disastrous Conflagration which ever happened in the United States. The wind was blowing hard from the South, which increased as the fire extended. At 9 o'clock it blowed a perfect gale. The fire extended more than a mile and one third reaching North Street on Munjoy [Hill], and averaging nearly 1/3 of a mile in width. Among the buildings destroyed was the City Building, 7 churches, 5 hotels, and all of the shoe and leather dealers, Houses on Union and Middle Streets, all of the whole sales dry goods Establishments on Middle Street, and the large Sugar House of Brown and Sons, and the machine and foundry shops of Charles Staples. It is estimated that 1,500 families were burnt out and two lives lost. The loss is estimated at $10,000,000, on which this is an insurance of about _____. There was Engines here from Saco, Biddeford, Brunswick, Bath, Gardiner, Augusta, and Lewiston, which rendered good service. Our own Engines worked well and came out in good order, but laboring under great difficulty on account of poor hose. The fire was finally stopped about 2 o'clock the afternoon of the 5ᵗʰ. The cause of the Fire was Fire Crackers.

Spencer Rodgers, Chief Engineer

On Friday, July 6, 1866, the *Portland Daily Advertiser* reported:

Wednesday, the Fourth of July, 1866, will never be forgotten in the annals of Portland. It was a day of terrible devastation and ruin—a day of mysterious Providential dealing such as no city ever before experienced. The night of the anniversary of the Nation's Independence, which was to be a day of mirth and enjoyment, was turned to a night of terror. The leaping flames came on, licking up houses after house, reaching up a forked tongue to engulf and devour. The citizens stood aghast. Petrification appeared on the countenance of every man, and the utter futility of human endeavors to arrest the destroyer was inscribed on the countenances of all. Portland was unprepared for such a calamity—The great desideratum was water. The wells and cisterns were drained early. Water, water, was the universal cry. The firemen on account of their almost superhuman exertions, were paralyzed. And yet the wall of fire walked on—no check anywhere: Portland was Doomed!

The city was deficient in fire apparatus—buildings were torn down by ropes, fire-hooks not being at hand. As a general thing the streams of

Fire!

water from the steamers were feeble and too few. The Fire Department of the city is below what it ought to be. It lacks zeal, daring and efficiency, and the blame is not with the firemen, for they are a hardy and brave set of men, but with the City Government. It has been niggard in its policy. The steamer sent to save the new City Hall got to work ten minutes too late. The attempts to blow up buildings was too long delayed, and when executed did no good. There seemed to be wanted a head to control matters.

On the flames came, seeming to gather increased wrath and devastation as they progressed. A rain of sparks covered the pavements, and the dry shingled roofs were again and again getting into a blaze. It seemed as though human effort was idle to save for a moment. Our beautiful city, our home, our delight, our pride, with its tree-lined streets, its magnificent dwellings, its churches and marts of trade, seemed to be selected on this eventful night as the victim of the dread fiat of the Almighty's wrath.

The fire swept completely through the city from the foot of High Street to North Street on Munjoy Hill, destroying everything in its tracks so completely that the lines of the streets can hardly be traced, and a space 1½-mile long by a quarter of a mile wide appears like a forest of chimneys with fragments of walls attached to them.

The wind was blowing a gale from the south and a tremendous sheet of flame swept along before it devouring everything in its passage, and the uttermost exertions of the firemen, aided by steamers and hand engines from several other places could only succeed in preventing it from spreading in new directions, many buildings—perhaps 50—were blown up, to check the flames.

The fire commenced in the Deguio's boat shop on Commercial Street and was caused by a lad firing a cracker among some shavings on the outside of the building, which set them on fire. The flames quickly communicated to the interior of the building, corner of Maple and Commercial streets also caught fire and rapidly burned.

There was a high wind prevailing at the time and the flames and cinders were blown directly upon the extensive buildings of the Portland Sugar House Company. Soon these were all on fire, and the large foundries of Messrs. Staples & Son, and N.P. Richardson on Commercial Street caught and though the most strenuous exertions were made to save them they were entirely destroyed. From these points the fire rapidly extended to York, Maple, and the lower part of Danforth Streets to Centre Street, destroying everything. From Centre Street it extended to Cotton Street, thence to Cross Street running up that street and extended down Middle street to

Temple and from Temple to Exchange street—from Fore street to the City Hall, and then down Myrtle to Cumberland street—from these bounds to India street, every building, save the Custom House is destroyed—on the north side of Fore street, both sides of Middle street, both sides of Federal street, both sides of Congress street, all on the south side of Cumberland street from Myrtle to Washington streets, except the Radford house on the corner of Pearl and Cumberland, together with all the buildings on the intersecting cross streets. The fire crossed Washington street and destroyed a large number of buildings between that point and North street. The flames blew over into Oxford street, and several dwelling houses were destroyed, and the flames are still raging. The building occupied by the Custom House and Post office was considered fire-proof. But the flames crept into the upper part of the building, occupied as a Court Room, and the interior was badly damaged. The Post-office part was not so much damaged and the mails were regularly made up there Thursday. It is estimated, roughly, at fifteen millions of dollars. So far as we have been able to learn there is insurance for upwards of $4,000,000. As to the names of the sufferers it is utterly impossible at this moment to give them. The heaviest losers are Hon. John B. Brown & Sons and Messrs. Churchill, Brown & Manson, who estimate theirs at about $1,000,000, on which there is insurance to the amount of $600,000.

This does not include the private buildings owned by Mr. Brown.

Eight Churches were destroyed; 1ˢᵗ Baptist, Federal Street; St Stephens Episcopalian, Pearl street; 2ⁿᵈ Parish, Middle street; Pearl street Universalist; Chapel of the Immaculate Conception, Catholic Church, Cumberland street; Swedenborgian, Congress street; Bethel, Fore street; 3ʳᵈ Parish, Congress street.

Eight hotels were destroyed—Elm, International, American, Commercial, Franklin, Kingsbury House, Sturdevant House and Freeman House. The unfinished marble hotel erected by the late Hon. John M. Wood, was burned down. The beautiful mansion of Mrs. Wood shared the same fate.

Every newspaper in the city was destroyed—There is no exception. The Advertiser, Argus, Press, Evening Star, Mirror, Transcript, Zion's Advocate, *and* Price Current *printing offices are gone.*

All the banks in the city, viz: 1ˢᵗ National, 2ⁿᵈ National, National Traders, Casco National, Canal National, Merchants' National, and Cumberland National were destroyed.

Fire!

Photo #1, taken July 6 near the corner of Congress and Franklin Streets, looking south. *John A. Whipple, photographer from Boston. Courtesy of Portland Fire Museum Collection.*

Every lawyers' office in the city was burned down—We believe there is not a single exception.

PROPERTY DESTROYED AFTER BEING REMOVED.

It was considered by every one that the City Hall would pass unscathed and consequently furniture and valuable articles were carried here for security—When the fire caught on the building there was hardly any time to remove them and a large portion was destroyed. Many persons also removed their furniture and goods to what they considered safe places; but the fire reached and destroyed them before the owners were aware of it.

Commercial Street.
From the coal office of Wm. H. Evans, near High street to Cotton street, every building on the North side was burned.

York Street.
Every building on the South side from High street to the Junction of Danforth street; and on the North side the three buildings next above Maple street, and all below Maple to Danforth.

Danforth Street.
All the buildings on the South side, from Maple to Fore streets, and all on the North side from the Gore House.

Center Street.
The brick building on the Western corner, and all the buildings on the Easterly side nearly up to Spring street.

Cotton Street
Three buildings on the West side, near Free street and six or eight on the other side of the street. The fire here did not extend up to Free street.

Cross Street
Both sides completely cleaned out from Free to Middle street.

Union Street.
All gone. All the shoe and leather shops, Winslow's foundry, Grant's coffee and spice factory and everything on both sides of the street.

Plumb Street
Every building on both sides gone. Among these, was the residence of Rev. Dr. Carruthers, and the building of the Portland Athenaeum.

Exchange Street.
A mass of ruins. Corey's great furniture establishment, all the bookstores, jeweler's shops, insurance offices and everything, save the Custom House, from Fore street to Congress street.

Lime and Milk Streets.
Every vestige swept away, including the Milk street and Warren markets. The fire extended clear through to Congress street.

Fire!

Temple Street.
Everything in ashes from Middle to Congress street.

Myrtle Street.
From Congress to Cumberland, nothing on the west side is gone but the City building. On the east side, all the buildings but the two lower ones were destroyed.

Fore Street.
With the exception of a block of three brick stores belonging to the estate of John Fox, every building on the north side of this street, from Centre to India street, is destroyed. On the south side of the street no buildings from Cross to India streets were touched.

Free and Middle Street.
The Free street block was destroyed, with the exception of the store owned by Mr. Tolford, and every building on Middle street, on both sides, from the junction of Free street to India street with the single exception of the store of Messrs. D.F. Emery & Sons, which is untouched, though the adjoining stores on both sides of this were destroyed. Here were all the principal dry goods establishments.

Federal Street.
The shop of Messrs. Marr Brothers and that of Dr. Mason, at the Junction of Federal and Middle streets, were saved. On the South side of Federal street, every building from Chase & Co.'s hardware store, to India street has gone. On the North side every building from and including the Elm House to India street shared the same fate.

Congress Street.
From Temple to India on the North side and from the City Hall to, and including the Catholic school house above Washington street, on the South side all in ruin.

Cumberland Street.
On the South side all the buildings from Myrtle to Washington street and thence above Washington street up Munjoy, are down. On the North side all the buildings from the Radford house, corner of Pearl street, are gone.

Photo #2, from the top of the Custom House looking south. *John A. Whipple. Courtesy of Portland Fire Museum Collection.*

Oxford Street.
In this street the fire was raging Thursday, but it was confined to the upper part, near Washington street. Several tenements were destroyed but we have not learned the number.

Other Streets.
In Silver, Willow, Vine, Deer, Chatham, Franklin and Hampshire streets every building was destroyed—The famous Sebastopol is among the things that are.

As we read John Neal's accurate account and his list of streets wiped out by the fire, we should remember an earlier quote from the city auditor's report of March 1866.

Fire!

Fire Department—*The expenditures in this department, including pay to companies and engineers of steam fire engine, have been $13,620.37, being a decrease from the previous year of $8,143.02. The department now consists of four steamers in full commission, one hook and ladder company, and one steamer held in reserve, ready for use in cases of emergency. Two hand engines have disbanded during the year, which, however, only accounts in part for the decrease of expenditure this year as compared with former years, a saving having been made in the ordinary expenses this year over those of last year of $7,771.32. This favorable result is largely due to the fact that there was a less number of severe fires than usual, and the department was relieved from the necessity of purchasing any new hose during the year.*

THE DISASTER AND
THE RESULTS

O n July 6, 1866, the *Portland Daily Press* reported:

The issues of the Portland Daily, Tri-Weekly Weekly Advertiser
*will be resumed as soon as new material can be obtained. The home of the
principal and city editor, the International Hotel, is in ashes, and refuge is
now on the street, with such assistance as kind friends give us. Our friend
may rely upon it that with us there is no such word as "failure," if you
trust, hope, persistency and determination will avail.*

*The track of demolition as we view it this morning is indeed a gloomy
picture. A highway of ashes and ruin is made through the city. People look
on and wonder at the extent of the terrible scene. But we are happy to see
so much spirit and alacrity. The man who talks of this being a blow from
which Portland cannot recover, talks wildly. It will not be so.*

*Such unconquerable courage and energy as speak out this morning, are
bound to succeed. Contracts have already been made for the erection of new
buildings, and the streets are being rapidly cleaned of rubbish.*

*The city of Portland, with a harbor of the very first character the world
can produce, and a country of great richness and fertility, at her rear;
Portland, the beautiful city of the east, will rise like Phenix from her ashes.
The adversity is of immense magnitude—almost overpowering—but no
true citizen of Portland will flinch for one moment. Now is the time for
action. If you ever had zeal, have it now. If you ever conquered adversity,
do it now. Talk hopeful—think hopeful—look hopeful—and act hopeful.*

Some thirty years ago the great commercial city of the country, New York, passed through an experience of terrific destruction by fire, of which this in Portland is an example. What was the result?

New York started anew on a race of enterprise from that very moment—the water of Croton River was turned into the city for future emergencies—and New York, from a position of mere commanding commercial influence became the great emporium of the Western world.

Energy. Stimulated under adversity, was the cause of this; and Portland, now under the hard experience of trial, smothered under the fire and brimstone of a hell of misfortune—under like energy will rise in true manhood and assert her merit and claims by the undaunted and unconquered able will of her citizens.

To expand on the number of streets rolled over by the fire, this further tally of streets was not included earlier:

Photo #3, from the corner of Congress and Lime (Market) Streets, looking north. *John A. Whipple. Courtesy of Portland Fire Museum Collection.*

The Disaster and the Results

ALL BUILDINGS DESTROYED:

Bank Street
Oxford Street
Harrison Street
Freeman Street
Chapel Street
Quincy Street
Locust Street
Montgomery Street
Larch Street
Bradley Lane
Stephens Court
Fox Court
Abysinian Court
Garden Lane
Freeman Place
York Place
Ingraham Court
India Court
Hancock Court

PARTIALLY DESTROYED:

Poplar Street
Anderson Street
Dyer Street
North Street
Boyd Street
Smith Street
Mayo Street
Wilmot Street
Sumner Street

Photo #4, City Hall at Congress and Myrtle Streets. *John A. Whipple. Courtesy of Portland Fire Museum Collection.*

This list was compiled by John Neal (1793–1876), known nationally as a writer, boxer, women's rights advocate and architect, who wrote extensively on the Portland conflagration. Neal wrote:

> *Our people were out by the thousands to see the balloon ascension, circus and trotting park, among them was the police force. Hence the unaccountable delay in giving the alarm which allowed the fire to get such headway.*
>
> *...Then came the crash of walls—the screams of women and children fleeing for their lives or huddling together at corners among their broken furniture and household goods—The blast of trumpets—the blowing up of buildings—heavy explosions—the fall of spires and churches, and huge warehouses, like the trembling battlement of a beleaguered city carried by storm.*
>
> *...Though the fire companies belonging to the city as well as others...labored hour after hour without quailing or flinching, in the midst of danger as great as*

that of the battlefield—with falling chimneys and tumbling walls and showers of broken slate and clouds of smoke and blazing cinders about them—scorching atmosphere that few could breath in safety...Our fire department was admirable and supposed to be efficient—with two or three exceptions perhaps—for every possible contingency and the highest praise from the first to last; many of them leaving all they had on earth to be destroyed, or pillaged while they occupied the fore front of the battle ground—acquitting themselves like men, together with the brave generous fellows from out of town...Steamers made eight or ten relocations each.

...It was reported, and believed for a time, that several companies were out of the city attending celebrations elsewhere, but the story had no foundation.

This notion was proven wrong by Neal shortly after the fire but is still alive.

Photo #5, from the top of the Custom House looking up Free Street. *John A. Whipple. Courtesy of Portland Fire Museum Collection.*

John Neal had an interest in the strength and adequate funding of the fire department as a citizen and property owner. His observations are well defined. He described the scene as a sweeping whirlwind of fire with inconceivable swiftness, of fire proof warehouses with iron shutters and slate roofs crumbling and falling in heaps before the terrific heat. This matches the description of a conflagration presented in the introduction of this text. Neal actually witnessed it and described it accurately. He wrote of the glass and metal being fused into molten masses, of a woman spending hours getting ready to move while her husband and friends carried water to wet the roof. She was later forced to "flee for her life." "She had just time to escape with her two children followed by her sister leading one little child and carrying one dead baby on her arm, the air so hot, it scorched her throat."

There were reports of other escaping people carrying corpses, all reported to be dead of various causes, prior to the fire. The only two fatalities attributed to the conflagration were Sabine Chickering and his mother.

Photo #6, from the top of Custom House looking west. *John A. Whipple. Courtesy of Portland Fire Museum Collection.*

Photo #7, City Hall, Myrtle Street side. *John A. Whipple. Courtesy of Portland Fire Museum Collection.*

John Neal observed:

I myself had an office on Exchange Street, far out of the range of the fire. It was protected on both sides by brick walls without a single opening and on one side was a vacant lot. In the rear was a new brick building only two stories high and all the back was fortified with iron shutters. Three times I passed that way in the course of an hour or two without an idea of being obliged to move my library and office furniture and only at last consented to open my safe.

...Within the next hour, that building together with the whole large block of stores and offices, running the whole length of Exchange Street to Middle Street was a pile of ruins and all the iron shutters they had put their trust in were shriveled like parchment and fluttering like old clothes on the cross wires.

At the great fire of New York in 1835—happening in mid winter, it did not seem so strange that granite should crumble and smolder though

I have known masses a foot square heated to a red heat and plunged into the sea at a temperature many degrees below zero, without crumbling or undergoing disintegration beyond the edges—yet here the whole broadside of that granite magnificent building, the Customs House, built of Quincy granite or sienite, more properly, flaked off, so as to resemble lime stone and the cornices and heavy projections were tumbling to the earth in fragments large enough to be very dangerous.

...And so it was everywhere—all the stone work, the granite, the gneiss the Albert stone, the slate, the sienite, all fared alike, all were transferred into shapeless, incandescent boulders and broken fragments.

The phenomenon that John Neal was describing is known as spalling, where the moisture in stone is heated to the point where it explodes. During

Photo #8, from Lime Street, looking southwest. *John A. Whipple. Courtesy of Portland Fire Museum Collection.*

the conflagration, firemen working at close range to the burning buildings were repeatedly pummeled by fragments of exploding stone.

A little family was gathered together, near a spot, where, only a few hours before, stood their happy home; the father, seated on a little heap of household stuff, which he had saved from the flames; and as he sat there his eyes fixed upon the ground, and twisting a fragment of stick between his fingers, his two half naked children at his knees, and wife standing before him, with large, silent tears rolling down her cheeks, trying to comfort him, it was really too piteous for description, and the spectator turned away speechless, and left them to look for consolation elsewhere. No less than thirteen dwelling houses which had escaped the fire of 1775, and outlasted all the changes since, were swept away by this.

The Portland Fire Department itself lost a great deal to the conflagration. Many lengths of hose were burned like fuses in the broiling streets. The wood-frame, two-story building of Casco No. 5 and the Washington Hook and Ladder No. 1 quarters at Congress Street at the head of Chapel Street were destroyed.

The two-story brick engine house of reserve Steam Fire Engine Falmouth No. 4 was destroyed on Congress Street near the head of Smith Street. The disabled Steam Fire Engine Casco No. 5 was stored inside of that building and was destroyed as well. A former hand engine house at Milk and Lime Streets was burned to the ground.

Portland mayor Augustus Stevens telegraphed Boston mayor Frederick Lincoln: "Thousands of our citizens are homeless and hungry in the streets. Can you send us some bread and cooked provisions?"

A train of five cars delivered provisions to ease the suffering of Portland on the fifth, contributed by the citizens of Boston. Captain Inman of the United States Army telegraphed for fifteen hundred tents. Hours later, a train loaded with supplies and many tents from the Union army pulled into Portland. The War Between the States had ended with the surrender of General Lee to General Grant at Appomattox only fifteen months before. President Abraham Lincoln had been assassinated six days after the April 9, 1865 surrender.

With these supplies, soup kitchens were set up in Market Square for those who were hungry and homeless. The army tents were set up on cleared ground, the largest section of which was at the Washington Street/Congress Street area at the foot of Munjoy Hill.

Most people had at least attempted to save their belongings from fire—silverware, clothing, the family Bible and other things that could be carried in their arms. The tents were pitched, and families took them over. Other people moved into private homes, which were filled to capacity. There were another six thousand people still on the streets.

The *Portland Fire Department Annual Report* of 1866–67, dated March 1, 1867, notes:

> *The disastrous fire which visited this city on the 4th day of July, whereby one third of all the buildings, and more than a third in value of all the property, was destroyed, and many thousands of our citizens were deprived of shelter and stripped of the savings of their whole lives in a single night, holds so leading a place in the history of great public calamities, that it is unnecessary for me here to report in detail upon it. The tabular statements*

Photo #9, from the top of the Custom House, looking southwest. *John A. Whipple. Courtesy of Portland Fire Museum Collection.*

of losses and insurance, appended to this report, exhibit all that I have been able to ascertain on these points, though much is undoubtedly omitted. The difficulties and accidents attending the commencement of this fire, cannot be known by those who had no share in the management of the department. And I shall only briefly allude to some of the more important, in the hope that misapprehension, so injurious to the interests of the citizens may be corrected. When the alarm was given, the wind was blowing violently in a direction to carry the flames upon combustible buildings and materials, as compactly placed as could be found in the city.

The fire commencing at the extreme windward side of the City and at the bottom of the hill, the wind drove the heat and sparks against the fronts of the buildings on the top of the hill. The season was very dry, and the buildings, heated by the sun, were ready to kindle from a spark of fire. The first engine that arrived, from some cause, would not take water.[25] The second and third after that arrived, lost much valuable time in consequence of bursting hose. Before the forth was ready to work, a second fire was reported to me on Union street, and she was sent to take care of that. It soon became evident to me that our fire department was inadequate to stop the fire, and appeals for help were telegraphed to Lewiston, Gardiner, Bath, Biddeford, Hallowell and Augusta, and a special train was sent to Saco.

Saco, Biddeford, Bath, Gardiner and Brunswick responded promptly that night and Lewiston and Augusta the next day, with men and engines to whose assistance we are greatly indebted for much that was saved.

Also, Chief Engineer Damrell, of Boston, sent a detail of men, from his department the next night, who rendered good service in relieving our almost exhausted firemen.

Before this relief could reach us, the fire was past control. All we could hope to do was to keep the extent of its course as narrow as possible. Small as the supply of water was, the firemen were driven from point to point, before it was exhausted. And the fire was blown by cinders to buildings far in advance of the place where the department was working; thus causing double the fires at one time that we had engines to meet them with. And each fire being a center from which other fires took, the extent of the burning district soon became so great, as almost to destroy communication between the board of engineers; and it was difficult to keep advised of the station of the engines at different points, and progress of the fire. So rapid was the extension of the fire, that before the engineers could reach any point to

Photo #10, from the top of the Custom House, looking south. *John A. Whipple. Courtesy of Portland Fire Museum Collection.*

employ the means in their possession, destruction had passed over it. All conditions were changed.

I am now, and always have been satisfied, that the only possibility of stopping the fire, would have been in having an engine at hand by the time the fire was discovered, and ready to work.

We cannot too strongly express our obligations to the firemen of the cities and towns above mentioned, for the ready help afforded us in our distress, for which our thanks were communicated by letter soon after the fire, in each case.

Let us hope that no community may ever stand in need of our assistance, while we assure them of our readiness to give prompt and active proof of our willingness, should any of them be so unfortunate as to require it.

I would return my thanks to Messrs. James Boyd and Son, of Boston, for their promptness and liberality in repairing for us free of charge, about 3000 feet of hose, and to the Steamboat Company, for free transportation.

The Disaster and the Results

I would also return my sincere thanks to Chief Engineer Damrell, of the Boston fire department, and also to Chief Engineer Breed, of the Lynn fire department, for their successful efforts, in their respective departments in supply[ing] us with 2000 feet of new hose immediately after the fire on July 4ᵗʰ.

Spencer Rogers, Chief Engineer

Chief Rogers does not, at any time in his official log or in his annual report to the city, lay blame or make excuses. He reports the facts as they are. The chief was almost prophetical in stating,

Let us hope that no community may ever stand in need of our assistance, while we assure them of our readiness to give prompt and active proof of our willingness, should any of them be so unfortunate as to require it.

Photo #11, a general view of the ruins from Munjoy Hill. *John A. Whipple. Courtesy of Portland Fire Museum Collection.*

On November 9, 1872, a conflagration tore through Boston.

Similarities prevailed between the Portland and Boston conflagrations. A delay in the alarm resulted when the discoverer of the fire was unable to locate a fire alarm box key holder to unlock the box and give the alarm. Key holders were residents near the box and the beat police patrolman. A twenty-minute search for a police officer permitted the fire to gain headway. A second contributing factor was a lack of water. The old water mains installed in 1849, twenty-three years previous, broke underground when a number of steam fire engines connected to the hydrants and began to pump large volumes of water. It was too much for the twenty-three-year-old system to handle. A third factor, unlike the case in Portland, was the further delay of the arrival of the fire companies. An epizootic was infecting the horses of a large section of New England. Unlike the case in Portland, the first responding apparatus was hauled, slowly, to the fire by men and boys. Most of the Boston Fire Department's horses were down with the disease.

The Portland Fire Department detailed Steam Fire Engine Machigonne No. 1 and a crew of firemen on a passenger train to provide mutual aid to Boston. The company connected oxen to the heavy steamer, since the Portland horses were all sick as well, and took the engine to a railroad bulkhead, where they loaded it onto a flatcar. Before arriving, according to Machigonne's engineer, Edward Porter, the train was stopped in Portsmouth by a conductor who did not approve of flatcars on passenger trains. The flatcar was shunted off, and the passenger train continued to Boston with the Machigonne crew. Boston was in a bad situation and could have used the Portland steamer.

Following the Portland conflagration, the *Daily Press* reported on July 7, 1866, that the reply for help Wednesday night was as prompt as the circumstances would allow:

Two engines from Saco arrived in forty five minutes after mayor Stevens telegraph was received. Lewiston sent on her steamer Liberty and about three hundred men…Both Brunswick and Gardiner, on their return from the celebration at Lewiston, got tidings from Portland at Brunswick and came to our aid with their hand tubs…From Augusta came the Fire Chief Engineer of the department with the steamer Cushnoc…Boston properly sent men to relieve our exhausted firemen.

The printers of the city, all burned out, met on Friday to discuss the availability—or, as they said, "getting up"—of a building for their print

Looking up Exchange from Fore Street, with the Custom House and City Hall in the distance. *J.P. Soule, #479. Courtesy of Portland Fire Museum Collection.*

offices. Usually in competition with opposing and diverse views on religion, politics and other subjects, they were now anxious to band together for the common cause of printing and distributing their editions.

An artist from *Frank Leslie's Illustrated Newspaper* in New York arrived by train at noon on Thursday and began sketching perspectives of the burned district. Wasting no time, he departed for New York on Friday.

The *Eastern Argus* of July 11, 1866, noted:

> *The report that a steam fire engine was surprised by the flames and burnt during the great conflagration, arose from the fact that the Casco being in a*

disabled condition and unfit for use, was not taken out and was destroyed with the building in which it stood. The old Cataract engine, which came from London, and has been in the department since 1802, was also burned. It had been preserved as a relic, but the firemen were too busy to save it.

The sixty-five-year-old hand engine was on display in the basement of City Hall. As we have already learned, Portland firemen, later assisted by the crew of the Boston Fire Department Steam Engine Company No. 10, operated inside the building, which was heavily involved in fire. Simultaneously, the blocks surrounding the City Hall were burning furiously and collapsing one after another. It was not the case that the "firemen were too busy to save it"; the companies were working incessantly to save it.

Within hours of the knockdown of the fire, special trains were arriving in the city bringing much needed food and clothing.

The City of Portland lost the aforementioned firehouses and the city building, also known as City Hall, plus Primary School #3, a two-story brick building; the single-story brick Primary School #13; and a two-story brick Boys Grammar School. The two-story brick Primary School #9 and Girls' Grammar School on Congress Street near the Eastern Cemetery was also destroyed.

Jacob Abbott, writing for the *Maine Normal*, noted:

After such a visitation as this, it was natural that the question on all lips should be, What shall we do? And inbued with that same spirit which so early led the Puritan Fathers to provide for the education of their children, the Fathers of Portland asked first of all, "What can we do for our schools?" Many of them had lost their buildings together with all their text books and apparatus, while others that were more fortunate in this respect, found that the children, as well as the men and women, were so thoroughly excited and appalled, that to attend to school duties and exercises was quite impossible. But a few days were sufficient in which to outlive this feeling; and a few days the Fathers of the town time enough to answer the question as to what should be done for the schools. The answer came firm and decided, as it always comes from every where in New England, when such a question is presented, "The schools must be the last to suffer." To the honor of Portland let it be recorded, that notwithstanding four school houses were destroyed, and eight schools left without rooms, and the city had met with such an unprecedented loss of property, within ten days all save three

Looking north from Fore Street at the foot of Exchange. *J.P. Soule, #481. Courtesy of Portland Fire Museum Collection.*

Primaries were reorganized and at work as usual; and ere the vacation, which was close at hand, had passed, these Primaries were provided with new temporary buildings. Some schools reopened with less than half their original number and without a text book of any kind. But amidst all this confusion and want, the teachers were not disheartened, for they opened before them an unusual field of usefulness. They went bravely about their work interesting and instructing the remnant of their scattered flocks, with no text book except the one the apt and skillful teacher always has in his possession. Thus they worked on, carrying the impression as much as possible that nothing had happened.

Portland City Hall. *J.P. Soule, #482. Courtesy of Portland Fire Museum Collection.*

On July 31, 1866, the *Portland Daily Press* printed the following:

THE PORTLAND FIRE DEPARTMENT

A day or two since a fireman stepped quietly into the Press office, and asked to have a brief communications put into the paper. At his direction the following lines were written down for that purpose:

When fire is cried and danger nigh,
God and the firemen is the cry:
But when quenched and all things righted,

The Disaster and the Results

God is forgot and the fireman slighted.
(signed) Portland Fireman.

We acknowledge the reproof. The newspapers of Portland have not yet done justice as they should, to the exertions of the fire department during the late conflagration. In excuses may we plead that no particulars of the services of the department have been furnished us, and that a thousand other matters have been constantly pressing upon our attention. By inquiring we learn that Portland steamer No. 2 was stationed most of the time on Centre street, and aided by the Falmouth on Cotton street, succeeded in preventing the fire from spreading further up town. The Cumberland rendered good service on Oxford street, and the Machigonne on Pearl street.

The hand engine Atlantic was manned by a company of volunteers and did good work. Many and well deserved thanks have been offered by the people of Portland to the fire companies which came from abroad to our assistance. It is time to recognize the fidelity and usefulness of our own firemen. All that fearful night and a good part of the next day they stood at their work, and dragged themselves wearily home at last for refreshments which nobody at that time had thought to provide. Their own houses perished, in several cases, while they remained at their posts. We shall gladly avail ourselves, whenever the official report is made up, of the opportunity to publish a fuller account of the service which at present we can only advert in a general way.[26]

Frank Merrill was a thirty-four-year-old longtime member and pipe man of Steam Fire Engine Company Machigonne No. 1. The nozzle is referred to as the "pipe," and pipe man is the position in the company that most enthusiastic firemen want to hold. Merrill responded with his company to the alarm on Commercial Street and recalled many years later:[27]

The old Machigonne engine put the first water on the sugar house and at first extinguished the flames which had then just got hold on the great structure. Then the water was turned on the boat shop and the last factory adjoining, part of the nest of wooden buildings in which the flames originated. It was at this time that orders came to change the position of the engine to York Street. As we went up Maple Street, said Mr. Merrill, the heat blistered the paint on the hose carriage and burnt off the line of hose lying in the street. The engine was then placed at the corner of High and Danforth Streets, the

Interior of City Hall. *J.P. Soule, #483. Courtesy of Portland Fire Museum Collection.*

hose leading down Danforth Street to Maple. The store house of the sugar refinery was then all on fire inside, but there were few openings in the walls, and they did not give way. We played on the houses on the opposite side of Danforth Street. It was so hot there that the only way we could work was by crouching behind a quilt which was held up as a screen by two men, and which we kept wet down with the house. We stayed there until 10 o'clock, and then went to the corner of Exchange and Federal Streets. We laid a line of hose down Temple Street almost to Middle Street, and played on the building where the Falmouth Hotel now stands.

You could look right through some of those buildings and see that everything on Union Street was at a white heat. Charles Day's Toy Store

Panoramic view of the burnt district, looking down Congress Street from Munjoy Hill. *J.P. Soule, #490. Courtesy of Portland Fire Museum Collection.*

was in the row of buildings on the site of the Falmouth Hotel. The wind was blowing a gale and all of a sudden, Day's stock of Fourth of July fireworks began to go off.

A big rocket whizzed over my head and then there came a regular volley. Perhaps you think I stayed there, but I didn't. I laid down that pipe, and ran. It was all I could do.

We chased along the edge of the fire and next came to a stand at Cumberland Street on the corner of Pearl. We ran the hose up Chapel Street at the head of which stood the old Third Parish Church. We worked on

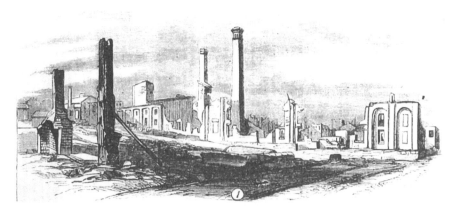

Drawing #1, the site of the boat shop where the fire commenced and the ruins of Brown's Sugar House. *Courtesy of* Frank Leslie's Illustrated Newspaper, *Portland Fire Museum Collection.*

the houses there and got the fire nearly out, but when the City Building got on fire it spoiled all we had done there. At five o'clock in the morning after I had been on the pipe twelve hours, I gave it up and went home. I believe that when the engine finally stopped work during the day of the fifth, it was down on the dump at the foot of Pearl Street, taking mud and water from the outlet of the sewer and playing it on the house roundabout.

Speaking of the way in which houses burned in that fire reminds me of something I was told. One man said he would time the burning of a house and watched Captain Tolford's, a large wooden house on Congress Street near Hampshire. The fire was then at its hottest, and it leveled that house in just seven minutes. The time was taken when flame first appeared on the building and it was just seven minutes to the time the house was down.

Mr. Merrill's experience is typical of that of many of the firemen, who after hours of hard service went home with singed hair, scorched faces and blistered hands.

Mr. Sterling, a former Portland police officer, remembered the fire:

When the fire first broke out, I went to the Sugar House and was there when that building caught fire. On the opposite side of Maple Street was a machine shop, and when the fire had worked its way into this shop it became terribly hot. Piled against the wall of the Sugar House were two tiers of hogsheads. The heat from the fire across the street set those hogs

The Disaster and the Results

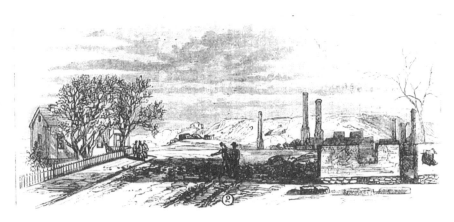

Drawing #2, McAllister's house on Washington and Oxford Streets, where the fire was finally checked. *Courtesy of* Frank Leslie's Illustrated Newspaper, *Portland Fire Museum Collection.*

heads burning. You know how such hogsheads will burn. The windows in the Sugar House, seemed to melt and fall in, and in a minute it was burning like powder. That's the way the Sugar House caught. I stayed near the Sugar House until the houses on Cotton Street were burning and an alarm was sent in for a fire on North Street. Two houses were burned down up there, and I suppose they caught fire from sparks from the great fire. I went to Cotton Street and worked carrying water from wells to put on the flames. There were lots of wells in the yards about the city in those days. Then I went to my house on Cumberland Street just above Green Street, and changed my clothes. I didn't get home again until the next day. We went to work moving goods from stores on Exchange Street to Post Office Square, boots, shoes, dry goods and anything we could find. They were all heaped in a pile and of course they were afterwards all burnt up. I went up to Purrington's Furniture Store on Exchange Street near Congress Street. We took a lot of the furniture from there and stored it in the basement of the City Building, where we thought it would be safe. It was near Purrington's that a lot of us saved one of the engines which had been abandoned. We got near enough to it to tie a rope to the rear axle and dragged it out of danger. Then we went to work to save the City Building.

I carried water from the cell room to the balcony on the front and from there we threw it against the front of the building to keep it cool. The International Hotel had stood opposite where the Davis Building now is. It had been burnt so low that we thought the danger to the City Building

Drawing #6, a general view of Portland city and the burnt district from the observatory on Munjoy Hill. *Courtesy of* Frank Leslie's Illustrated Newspaper, *Portland Fire Museum Collection.*

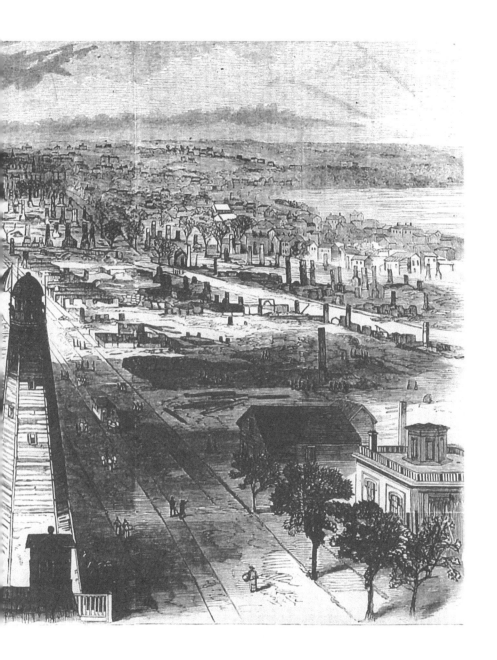

was over but it caught away up under the coping some hours later, and the fire burned though into the attic. I was in the building when it caught. The cells were unlocked and the prisoners which had been arrested during the day had been released; that is all but one of them. About 10 o'clock the next forenoon, I was at the building, then mostly in ruins, when I heard a cry. I crawled over the piles of brick into the cell room, and found a man in cell 15. He had been forgotten when the cells were unlocked, and he had stayed where he was while the building burned ever and around him.

The cell was on the west side of the room, and he got air, the high wind blowing into the room through an open window. The cell room, then as now, was partly finished in wood laid on brick and iron. The door to the patrolman's room and that to the yard had been burned out, and the woodwork in the east corridor of the cell room had been burned, but the man was not even scorched, thanks to that window, the high wind and the fact that he was on the west side instead of the east.

When the City Building caught, Archibald Montgomery, who was then a policeman, was in the dome looking for fire. He came downstairs on the run, but his whiskers were scorched as he ran through the blazing attic.

Mr. Sterling related another story:

Deputy Marshal Alanzo Wentworth, Ruel Field and I started from the City Building at about six o'clock. We had two kegs of powder in the team, and I was lying holding a blanket over it, while sparks and flying brands rained down on us. We drove to Hugh Carney's house on Fore Street near Plum. Then the fire was ripping along towards us. It had reached Cross Street. We put in one of the kegs of powder, set a fuse to it and touched it off. It did its business very completely. We also blew up the Blazier house on Plum Street.

That wasn't the only way that was tried to stop the fire by removing buildings. Before we tried the powder, Captain Jacob McLellen sent me to Lyman & Richardson's for a coil of hawser. I got it and a kedge anchor, and then we took the outfit to the Richardson Wharf property on Commercial Street, where there were a number of small buildings. Captain McLellen was a man who could give orders and take the responsibility and people would work under him. We would throw the anchor over one of these buildings and then a hundred men would get hold of that hawser and pull all together. The line of men would reach clear across Commercial Street.

Drawing #8, the U.S. Custom House and Post Office building with the ruins of the City Building in the background. *Courtesy of* Frank Leslie's Illustrated Newspaper, *Portland Fire Museum Collection.*

We tore down ten or fifteen small buildings in this way and I believe that to have saved Commercial Street below that point.

The loss amounted to $15,000,000, with fifteen hundred buildings destroyed and two fatalities. Churches, very important and personal to people, were destroyed, including: First Baptist, St. Stephen's Episcopal, Second Parish Congregational, First Universalist, Immaculate Conception Catholic, New Jerusalem, Swedenborgian, Bethel Free Congregational and Third Parish Congregational.

LESSONS LEARNED

It seems that the Portland conflagration of 1866 should have been a catastrophic event by which lessons were learned. Over decades and centuries, firemen in Portland have proven themselves—by their actions and through their judiciousness in spending town and city funds. In the hand engine era, a pumper costing $500 was worked hard and taken proper care of, often lasting twenty years or more. Firemen washed and cleaned the equipment and apparatus following each run. They scrubbed the wheels to remove dirt and horse manure while checking for damage to the wheels, axles and the pumper. They also did much of the labor in and around the firehouse, resulting in a reduced cost, or no cost, to taxpayers. This firefighter tradition continues today.

Time is always against the firefighter. In the case of the 1866 conflagration, this battle of time is compounded by or with a severe lack of experienced firemen, sufficient numbers of apparatus and firefighting equipment and an appropriate supply of water. The effect of these factors is that, in a short time, fire will extend, multiply and grow. Because no horses were provided exclusively to the fire companies, teams had to be located and brought to the engine houses, connected to the apparatus and started on the run.

Portland had evolved into a fine, busy city. Both plain and ornate well-designed buildings lined the streets. Cozy homes and energetic commercial and mercantile buildings were owned and occupied by taxpayers, who expected and deserved protection from the forces of fire. The new City Hall building had just been completed—a beautiful and ostentatious four-story building with an octagonal dome and an attached theater-style auditorium. The hard-earned taxpayer dollars, spent on elegant civic buildings and celebrations, may be satisfying to some segments of residents, but when that vital protection from fire is needed at the moment and is less than adequate or insufficient, all satisfaction disappears and is replaced by fear and tragedy.

Time is always against the firefighter. All major fires begin with a tiny spark. Firefighters have long asserted, "The first five minutes are worth the next five hours." The efficiency of firefighters preparing for the run and the emergency resulted in reduced lost time. The speed of the fire alarm office receiving and transmitting the alarm; the slide pole invented by a fireman to quickly get from the second- or third-floor living quarters to the main floor; bells and sirens to warn traffic and clear the way for responding apparatus; the quick hitch for the horse-drawn pieces; and electric door releases installed in the nineteenth century to open horse stall doors, apparatus doors and slide pole doors all contributed to the reduction of time between the discovery of fire and the prompt arrival of firefighting units.

The often heard, or read, quip "By the time the fire department got there"—usually used in a pejorative manner—indicates that firemen arrived late. Time is always against the firefighter.

In his annual report of March 1, 1867, Chief Rogers wrote:

To the Honorable City Council:

There has been added to the department since the July fire, one steam fire engine, at a cost of $4,500, to take the place of No. 5, which was disabled at the Temple Street fire, and which after being examined, was condemned, and stored in the engine house on Congress near the head of India Street [Smith Street], *and finally destroyed at the great fire on the 4th of July.*

There has been added to the department the past year, 400 feet of rubber hose, 2,250 feet of double riveted, and 1000 feet of single riveted hose, at a cost of $7,274; and I would recommend to your honorable body the purchase of at least 4000 feet more. We have, beside the above mentioned, about 7100 feet, most of it is weak and in poor condition, and I doubt if there is 2000 feet of it that will stand more than one hundred pounds pressure, and as in consequence of the imperfect supply of water, we are often required to play through long lines of hose—sometimes 1400 feet, the hose is subjected to great strain, and frequently bursts at critical moments, causing the loss of much valuable time, when the water is most needed.

Each engine runs about 1000 feet of hose to fires, and requires as much

Casco Steam Fire Engine No. 5, purchased after the conflagration from the Portland Company in 1866 to replace Casco No. 5's engine, which was destroyed in the Congress Street Engine House at the head of Smith Street (also destroyed). *Courtesy of Portland Fire Museum Collection.*

more to change. It will appear plain from this statement, that the supply of hose is much less than is demanded for the good condition of the department.

The purchase of a carriage that will carry 1000 feet of hose, to be run to fires, to supply the department with spare hose, is recommended. There has been contracted for, and will soon be delivered, a new hook and ladder truck at a cost of $750. I would suggest that the old carriage be hauled to fires by horse, one company to take charge of both trucks at fires, which, in my opinion, will make this branch of the department all that is needed for the present.

There has been contracted for, and will soon be completed, a fire alarm telegraph, at a cost of $5,300, which in time saved, and also by giving the locality, will be of great benefit in extinguishing fires. I would recommend to your honorable body, the purchase of a bell of at least 10,000 lbs. weight, to be placed on the new city hall, to be used in connection with the telegraph, whereby the citizens as well as firemen, may know the locality, and the alarm of fire may be promptly and widely given.

There has not been any money expended the past year to increase the supply of water, and if there is no prospect of water being introduced into the city within a short time, I would recommend that a reservoir be built on the corner of Pine and Carlton streets, and the reservoir at the corner of Brackett and Pine streets be enlarged, to make it of the first class. Also, that those at the corner of Union and Middle, and the corner of Exchange and Middle streets, be altered into cisterns, and the water taken from the surrounding buildings; and that the two reservoirs on Commercial street, be cemented, and pipes laid to high water mark, to keep them supplied, which will make them of some benefit. In their present condition they are almost useless.

I would suggest that there be procured near Commercial street, some place to keep a supply of fresh water and coal, for the use of the engines, when working at salt water.

I would also recommended to your honorable body the purchase of three horses, to be kept in the new engine house stable, to haul the engine and hose carriage to fires in day time as well as at night; as it is often the case, that the horses, now employed, are a long distance from their engines when the alarm of fire is given in the day thereby causing great delay.

I am very well aware, gentlemen, that the suggestions I make, if adopted by you, will cost considerable; and I have come to the conclusion that it is impossible to keep this department in a high state of efficiency without a larger expenditure of money than has been unusual heretofore.

In various departments of the city government, in my opinion, there is none that demand more serious consideration, than a well paid and efficient fire department, and no other so essential to the lives and property of our citizens.

I am happy to inform your honorable body, that No. 5 and hook and ladder company, are permanently located in the new building on the corner of Congress and Market streets. The second story, over the engine house, is finished for a dwelling for the engineman, which will be of great advantage to the department, beside being a source of income to the city. And I would recommend that rooms over other engine houses be finished for the same purpose.

The chief's request for hose for the carriages and hose for change refers to the necessity to pack one thousand feet of two-and-a-half-inch leather hose on the reel for fire duty and have another one thousand feet in reserve for replacing the hose when it's wet and must be dried in the heated hose tower. Care for the leather hose had always been done following each use at a fire. It was cleaned, oiled to keep it flexible and rolled to store in the engine house. The apparatus and equipment had been well maintained by the firemen since the late 1700s. They recognized that if they took care of the equipment, it would take care of them. This practice has been substantiated by the long duration of the hand engines in service: twenty, thirty or more years.

This plan would place the new truck, equipped with 162 feet of ground ladders, and the older 1839 truck, carrying five ladders of 140 feet total, on the fire ground. The new Steam Fire Engine Casco No. 5 was a J.B. Johnson, four-hundred-gallon-per-minute pumper built by the Portland Company on the waterfront.

A new firehouse was constructed in 1867 at Congress Street and Market Street—a two-and-a-half-story attractive building with a cupola. Engine Company No. 5 ran from a bay on the 376–382 Congress Street side. Washington Ladder Company No. 1 was quartered on the 133

The new Casco No. 5 Engine House at the corner of Congress and Market Streets, built after the fire and completed in 1867. Washington Ladder Company No. 1 was quartered on the Market Street side. *Courtesy of Earle G. Shettleworth, Maine Historic Preservation Committee.*

Washington Hook & Ladder No. 1, ordered from Remington & Moulton Co. of Providence in 1866, arrived in 1867 after the conflagration. *Courtesy of Portland Fire Museum Collection.*

Market Street side. Living spaces were provided on the second floor for the firemen.

An order was passed on November 19, 1866, for the purchase and installation of a fire alarm telegraph system, which had been investigated five years previous. The fire alarm office was located on the second floor of this firehouse. The system included twenty-six stations, or street boxes, connected to the office by eight and a half miles of wire, gongs at each firehouse and two church bells connected with strikers—one at the First Parish Church at Congress Street at the head of Temple Street, and the other at St. Stephen's Church at Congress Street and Avon Street.

Levi L. Cummings, former fireman and driver of Machigonne's hose reel carriage, was appointed fire alarm superintendent.

Most of these improvements, authorized by the city government, had been requested or recommended by the chief engineers in years previous to the conflagration. A two-and-a-half-story brick engine house was built at 99 India Street near Congress Street in 1869. This house would eventually house Steam Fire Engine No. 4.

Work commenced throughout the burned-out sections soon after the fire was extinguished. Men collected and cleaned bricks for reuse. Streets were cleared and widened. Refuse was disposed of.

In a short time, John Neal was observing a great city with an inspiring attitude:

Already, more than three hundred buildings are in advanced progress, and not a few occupied by carpenters, painters, furniture dealers, grocers and small traders, while hundreds more give promise of speedy occupation by our largest wholesale dealers.

One hundred and twenty families have been lodged in barracks and forty eight more will get in during the week. There are forty-four tenements on the Hill, forty eight on the "Dump," thirty-one near the Glass Works, and fifty-four near the Workhouse, almost done. All these accommodations are in addition to the great number which the Committee have aided individuals to put up.

The *Eastern Argus* of June 15, 1867, reported:

FIRES—The fire epidemic seems still to rage. Almost every day some new disaster from the devouring element is chronicled. There is doubtless a considerable percent of the fires due to incendiarism but far more to the carelessness of individuals. A large proportion of the damages done is due to the neglect to provide suitable apparatus to extinguish fires and to keep heat apparatus in order. The engineers of a Hartford steam engine which went to fight fire at Tarifville and save carpet factories says: "A steam fire engine when the fire first broke out would have subdued the flames and saved nearly all of the property." This is undoubtedly correct, providing the engine were in good order and supplied with strong hose; But if the engines were disabled as was one of the Portland engines when the great fire occurred; or if it was supplied with rotten hose as was the case with our fire engines a year ago, the presence of an engine would not have saved the property. Had the Falmouth been supplied with decent hose last 4th of July there would have been no great fire in Portland. She would have completely drowned the fire out in 20 minutes after she was on the ground had not her hose been too rotten for use and given out almost immediately.

Chief Spencer Rogers reported in 1867:

The telegraph has worked very satisfactorily and has rendered incalculable service to the department. As under the old arrangement of giving the alarm of fire the time consumed to enable the steamer to proceed to the fire and ready to play, was from fifteen to twenty minutes. With the present faculties the steamers are ready to work from ten to fifteen minutes from the time the alarm is given and in some cases less time.

Unfortunately, it took the destruction of one-third of this great city to arrive at that conclusion.

To afford a fire break in the heart of the city, an open space designed to at least slow any future conflagrations, the blocks were cleared and a fine Victorian-style park was constructed, boarded by Federal, Pearl, Congress and Franklin Streets. In commemoration of Portland's rising from the ashes, it was named Phoenix Park. The name was later changed in honor of assassinated president Abraham Lincoln.

In the annual report of 1868–69, Chief Engineer Franklin Moody stated in part:

Hose House—In September last, I sent a communication to the City Council, in reference to the absolute necessity of having a suitable house for this purpose, the present one is not at all adapted for the convenience of cleaning and drying hose; but no action was taken upon my recommendation. It frequently occurs that from five to seven thousand feet of hose is used at one fire, and the time consumed, to clean and dry it, is from ten to fifteen days, to have it ready for use.

With proper facilities for this purpose, the time and expense would be very much reduced. The average expense for this work, for the past two years, has been $900.00 per year. I earnestly recommend that a suitable house should be built for that purpose, in a convenient locality.

Hook and Ladder Company—In this branch of the department, which is a very important one an additional supply of extension ladders has been added, which was much needed, as the buildings erected since the fire of July 4th, 1866, are much larger and higher than formerly. The ladder truck has been altered to receive them, and we shall soon have a sufficient supply of ladders for that purpose.

Engines—Steamers Nos. 2, 3, and 5 are in good condition, and reliable. Steamer No. 1 Machigonne, has been in service longer than either of the others. This engine was the first one that was purchased for the city in 1859. Repairs have been made upon her from time to time, but is not considered reliable, and may give out at the time when most needed. I recommend that a new engine should be purchased to take her place. Even when we have our "Water Works" completed, I deem it for the interest and protection of the city to have not less than FOUR reliable steamers in service, ready for any contingencies which may arise.

Following the conflagration, the amount of money spent on repair of hose was $741.67; $5,974.94 was allotted for the purchase of new two-and-a-half-inch leading leather hose.

In May 1868, the recently organized Portland Water Company began laying sixteen miles of pipe from Sebago Lake to supply the hydrants and domestic water to Portland. The lake was 267 feet above sea level. The Portland mains of four, six, ten, twelve, sixteen and twenty inches supplied the sixty-five Lowery hydrants and seventeen Johnson Post hydrants. The hydrant pressure on Commercial Street, the lowest in the city, was at first sixty pounds per square inch but was then increased to ninety pounds. This pressure was ample to supply the steam fire engines. The project was slated for completion on July 4, 1869, a great step forward in fire protection in the city.

The ten-million-gallon reservoir, nearly the capacity of reservoirs in East Boston and South Boston combined, was completed on Bramhall Hill on November 18, 1869, supplying hydrants in the city. In 1870, the hydrant contract for $4,000 was signed.

As decimated blocks were being cleared for rebuilding, old narrow streets that traced ancient footpaths were straightened and widened for reconstruction, which commenced soon after the fire was extinguished. Many brick buildings constructed on the sites formerly occupied by nests of wooden buildings and smaller brick structures were designed and built to four and five stories, with fire walls and slate roofs. The architecture was mostly Victorian, employing both brick and iron decoration.

Middle Street was all new construction. Some buildings were brick covered with mastic, some were pressed brick, and there was wide use of granite for lintels, doorways and caps and sills. Styling varied from Baroque Revival to Greek Revival, with Italian and French influences, with roofs of gambrel, flat, gable and hipped styles. These varied styles all blended in harmony with one another and with the nearby surviving pre-conflagration Colonial-style buildings.

The following is an excerpt from the mayor's address to the city council in 1869–70:

Fire Department—Your attention is particularly invited to the report of the Chief Engineer of the Fire Department. Since the fire of 1866, this department has been greatly improved, and its efficiency demands our special notice. But I am advised by those who, by their intimate

Portland City Hall, rebuilt after the conflagration. *Courtesy of Maine Historical Society.*

knowledge of the facts are more competent to form an intelligent judgment, that much yet remains to be done to make the workings of the system perfect. I commend the subject to your consideration, merely remarking that over careful saving in the department may prove in the end to be practical wastefulness. Our firemen stand on guard day and night, in storm and sunshine, against the most dangerous enemy to our prosperity, as we have had single occasion to know, putting in peril both health and life. The people can well afford to acknowledge this service, not by complimentary words alone, but by adequate and substantial remuneration.

Chief Engineer Franklin Moody reported in March 1870:

Steam Fire Engines—We have in the Department four Steamers, which are all in good condition and reliable. The steamers "Falmouth" and "Machigonne" have been sold to the Portland Company, and the city have purchased a new Engine of the first class from the same company, which is located in the Engine House on Brackett street and designated as "Cumberland, Steamer No. 3." The Engine formerly known as No. 3, is now located at the Engine House on Congress street near Oak street, and is now designated as "Machigonne , No. 1" with the same company attached to her as formerly.

It was common to purchase a piece of apparatus, place it in a company and then reassign that company's engine to another company that was running an older piece.

Chief Moody's report continued:

Hose House—The large two story brick building located on South Street, has been converted into a Hose House for the storage of the Hose belonging to the Department, and also for the purposes of cleaning, drying and repairing hose and is well adapted for that purpose. The building is seventy three feet long and nineteen feet wide. The tower is fifty feet high, and eleven feet by seventeen and a half in width, and will contain five thousand feet of hose.

At the present time we have blocks and pulleys for three thousand five hundred feet of hose, and with the present facilities we can clean and dry the hose in thirty six hours. While under the old arrangement, the time consumed in some cases, would be at least from two to three weeks. All repairs on hose is now made by Mr. Levi J. Cummings, superintendent of hose house.

The comparison of Portland to Boston is seen in a few instances. The town and city of Portland was similar in a few ways to the town and city of Boston. Both were seaports. Both were situated on a major river with a harbor and a body of water to the back for the town, back cove or Back Bay. Both were cities of narrow streets, alleys, places and courts. Both were the scenes of battles with tribesmen and English soldiers. Both had similar fire hazards and building construction and adopted ordinances and laws to address them. Boston was older and somewhat larger in size and population, and with the larger tax base, so it was more advanced in its ability to purchase fire apparatus and equipment. Since the days of hand-drawn engines, a strong camaradeship has existed between firefighters of the two cities.

By 1874, John Neal was writing glowingly of a particular renewed section of the city. Exchange Street and the immediate area had been rebuilt in first-class order:

We have now along both sides of this attractive and busy thoroughfare, large, handsome blocks and warehouses, of granite, iron, Albert stone, pressed brick and common brick, three and four stories high, with mansard roofs, and large halls and chambers, adapted to the wants of a manufacturing region. These buildings are all, upon the average, fifty or sixty feet to the eaves, well slated roofs, large, dry and well lighted cellars, deep drainage, and generally water closets, sinks and Sebago water; and also—a fact worth recording—with a reasonable amount of architectural embellishment, heavy cornices, rich windows, and pilasters to correspond. Instead of being only thirty five or forty feet in depth, most of these are from eighty to one hundred and twenty, or even here and there, one hundred and fifty feet in depth, and they are generally finished within, after a superior style, with our richest native woods, black and yellow ash, maple and walnut, oiled and varnished. The floors are laid with southern pine, the cellars with heavy plank or cemented, and all are now occupied for banking houses, brokers' offices, insurance offices, auction rooms, bookstores, warehouses and manufactories.

The ground floor is almost always stuccoed, the ceilings frescoed, with handsome cornices, and the windows of large plate glass. But enough may be seen at a glance, to satisfy all that a wonderful improvement in the style of architecture, and in all the ornamentation has taken place, to say nothing of the great additional conveniences, the greater safety—not a single wooden building is there now on the street, nor in the neighborhood…and the Sebago water, which goes up almost of itself to the mansard roofs and attics of our highest buildings.

This was the heart of the mercantile and financial district of the city and the state, and the new buildings were perfectly matched for the purpose. Jacob Abbott wrote in March 1867:

Portland is beautiful in its ruins, because it has a beautiful situation. But it can hardly be said now to be "in ruins." It is to have a new life, and better than it has ever known. Portland is to be the Queen of the East. Manufacturers, trade, commerce are to flourish here as hardly elsewhere upon this continent. This is to be the metropolis of the "ever fresh and vigorous Orient." The enterprise of her business men can no longer be called in question. Blocks of stores, that would be a credit to any age and any city, have risen since the "Great Fire" as if by the wave of a magician's wand. Old enterprises have been revived, and new ones begun. The city is full of life. The young are busy, and will amass fortunes. The old renew their youth, for they must see the old home populous and thriving again. Ere they lay their armor down. Old grudges and differences "went up" in the conflagration. New capital will be invited. And better men, stronger physically, intellectually and normally, will grow out of this city's hour of trail.

EPILOGUE

The main floor looks pretty good now. The curator hung up the dry mop. Yes, if the docents had the time to relate the story of the conflagration properly, they would probably tell it something like that.

When the more thoughtful guests ask, "Could it happen again?" the docents sometimes make comparisons.

Could Portland be seriously damaged by another conflagration? Residents of Portland know that it is not unusual for wind exceeding thirty-five miles per hour to blow from the harbor into the city. Firefighters recognize that the hydrant system is reliable; however, at certain major fires, it has been necessary for the water supply chief to set up fire engines to pump from hydrants on larger mains in order to provide sufficient water for the engines using hydrants on smaller or damaged water mains closer to the fire. The hydrant system lost water in October 1996 due to storm damage to major portions of the supply system. This left 140,000 customers without domestic water and the fire department without operating hydrants. Within forty-eight hours, with little or no water pressure at the hydrants, the Portland Fire Department responded to 160 alarms. Firefighters worked fast and depended on the apparatus water tanks.

An ice storm in January 1998 froze hundreds of hydrants. Companies responded to 180 alarms within twenty-four hours, including three serious structural fires. Frozen hydrants cause delays in water supply. The hydrants are reliable but subject to the forces of nature.

Although it may not be readily recognizable, firefighters and insurance companies know that there are thousands of combustible buildings in

Portland. There are buildings of fire-resistant construction, but none, regardless of how substantial, is capable of holding back extensive fire. The stated action of intense heat breaking windows and instantly igniting building contents is still possible and is a phenomenon that will not change.

The question may arise, keeping in mind lessons learned from the 1866 conflagration: are there a sufficient number of engine and ladder companies? To answer this question, the evolution and devolution of the fire department must be studied.

In 1955, the Portland Fire Department consisted of nine engine companies and a six-thousand-gallon-per-minute ninety-foot fireboat. Five ladder companies were situated throughout the city. A heavy rescue unit was also in service responding citywide.

The center of the city, the downtown area shopping district, the warehouse section and the waterfront were known by the National Board of Fire Underwriters and by the fire department as the "Congested Value District." This area was considered to be an irregular shape on the city map, consisting of forty-six blocks and including 474 buildings, exclusive of sheds and additions. This district was bordered by Cumberland Avenue and Oak, Shepley, Casco, Myrtle, Pearl, Federal, Church, Commercial, Cross, Free, Cotton and High Streets. It covered approximately ninety-one acres.

The Board of Fire Underwriters' report states:

> Large or excessive fire areas are found in all but thirteen blocks. The predominance of the fire resistivly weak buildings of ordinary construction makes individual fires probable, which can readily extend through unprotected window and communicating openings the adjoining buildings and possibly involve an entire block. In the older section of the district, combined with the severe exposure from the wharf area, provide a tendency for a fire to sweep up toward the concentration of high value along Congress Street.
>
> The wharf and pier district extends from State Street to Waterville Street, extended. Buildings are grouped frames some iron clad interspersed with a few of ordinary construction. Although heights are generally low, areas in some instances are large to extensive, and interiors of the larger piers are poorly accessible. Storage of highly combustible materials is prevalent, and although areas that are sprinklered have increased, fire protection features are mainly lacking. Severe unfavorable conditions might readily sweep the district.

The warehouse district and waterfront were determined by the insurance underwriters to be high hazard districts. The buildings in these districts, by the 1930s and the Great Depression, had been used for many purposes with minimal maintenance. Hundreds of broken windows, poorly kept wood-frame buildings and closely built structures with vast open spaces posed a conflagration hazard.

The report stated, "The wharf and pier area is still depreciating and severely exposes the congested value district thereby offering a serious conflagration hazard."

In 1955, the Portland Fire Department was organized into nine engine companies. Those in the Congested Value District, Engine Companies 5, 2, 4 and 1 were manned with four, five or six firemen on duty. Other engine companies were staffed with four. Ladder Company No. 5 and Ladder Company No. 1, both in that district, ran with four or five men each. Proper manning was of interest to the insurance companies due to the severe conditions under which the firemen operated, including heavy hoses. A charged hose line of two hundred feet weighs four hundred pounds, while ground ladders are four or five hundred pounds. It requires many trained firemen to handle these and other equipment. The rescue and removal of a human from fire takes many firefighters to safely accomplish. Engine Company No. 7, the six-hundred-gallon-per-minute fireboat, was staffed with five men. A reserve high pressure hose wagon was available to operate with the fireboat. The boat could moor to a wharf to pump, and the hose wagon could lay hose from the boat up into the congested value district. This was done in 1908 for a major fire at Middle and Market Streets.

In the city of Portland, company response to alarms of fire was heavy out of necessity, due in part to the predominant building construction. Upon the first alarm, when a fire alarm box was pulled, three engine companies, two ladder companies and the rescue responded.

When in the judgment of the first arriving company officer or chief additional companies were required, a second alarm was ordered. The response to the second alarm was two more engine companies and a ladder company. When the fire was of such magnitude that the companies operating or responding to the fire were unable to handle the situation, the third alarm was transmitted, bringing two more engine companies to the fire, as well as a ladder company. The fourth alarm was struck when more help was needed and brought two more engine companies. The level of alarms was always predicated on the size of the fire, life hazard, exposure, weather conditions, water main size and proper manning. For example:

Box 423, Middle & Free Streets	Engine 5-1-4, Ladder 1-5, Rescue 1
Second Alarm	Engine 2-6, Ladder 3
Third Alarm	Engine 8-11, Ladder 6
Fourth Alarm	Engine 9-3

When a second alarm was struck, the off-duty firemen were required to respond to the fire, thus providing additional men at the fire. The department was made up of 176 men working a two-platoon system, with a seventy-four-hour workweek. The Board of Fire Underwriters noted in its conclusions that "manning is considerably deficient, particularly during vacation periods."

Within this Congested Value District was a certain area of conflagration hazard blocks, bounded by Federal, Middle, Temple, Milk, Fore, Pearl and Market Streets. From the view of the firefighters and the insurance underwriters, these were the highest conflagration hazards.

One example within the high-congested district cited in the Fire Underwriters' report was:

> *The block bounded by Boothby Square, Milk, Pearl and Silver Streets. A small irregular block is solidly built up with 1- to 4-story frame buildings and three ordinary buildings of 1 to 4 stories each. Occupancies include a paper box and candy factory, glass and furniture storage and printing. A fire gaining headway in any one of the large buildings could very easily sweep the block.*

The term "ordinary" denotes a type of construction of interior wood frame and noncombustible exterior walls.

The report then shifts to a distant neighborhood of concern, in the area bordered by Cumberland Avenue, Washington Avenue, Fox Street and Pearl Street:

> *One section called Bayside District, borders upon the Congested Value District. This section is in poor condition and the city has banned additions or major repairs to any building located therein with the ultimate objective of complete redevelopment, a plan for which has already been prepared. The majority of buildings are frame and a severe fire could readily spread to the congested value district.*

These pockets of compact, poorly maintained, derelict buildings were known as "conflagration breeders."

The Board of Fire Underwriters report recommended a number of improvements to the fire department, including:

That additional men be provided also that there will be at all times, including vacation periods, 7 men in high value pumper and ladder companies, and 5 men in other pumper and 6 men in other ladder companies, except the combination pumper and ladder company (Quad 3) which should have 8 men at all times.

In 1958, the Fire Underwriters issued a supplement to the 1950 report noting that the membership of the department numbered 208 and that the workweek had been decreased to sixty-three hours. With each reduction of hours, additional men were required to fill positions.

Museum guests are surprised to learn that the firefighter's workweek, although many hours, was all straight time. No overtime was paid.

In February 1973, the Insurance Services Office completed a report that performed the survey formerly conducted by the Fire Underwriters. The report acknowledged the department, consisting of 244 members with 23 non-firefighting positions. The firefighters average workweek was 50.4 hours.

Off-duty members now responded to third alarms, rather than the second alarms; however, they were not required to do so. The department was now composed of eight engine companies, one fireboat of seven-thousand-gallons-per-minute capacity, four ladder companies, one heavy rescue and one pumper on Peaks Island with two men on duty. In this report, it was also recommended:

1. That the owners of defectively constructed buildings which involve a serious life hazard or are so located as to form conflagration breeders be required to protect floor, fire wall, and exposed window openings.
2. That approved automatic sprinkler equipment be required in all basements exceeding 2500 square feet in area used for mercantile purposes and in all buildings which by reason of their size, construction, or occupancy involve a life hazard or may act as conflagration breeders.

This was a recommendation based on actual events. Between 1867, when rebuilding was begun following the conflagration of 1866, and 1972, there were, within the streets of the Congested Value District, more than 448 major building fires, some involving multiple buildings. There were many more such fires on the outside fringes of the district's perimeter.

Epilogue

The Insurance Services Office Report also noted:

That at least 5 members, including an officer, be on duty at all times with each engine and ladder company. (Note: Six members on duty, at all times with each engine and ladder company is considered standard manning.)

On January 22, 1960, Ladder Company No. 5 was decommissioned. On April 16, 1964, Engine Company No. 2 was decommissioned. On January 28, 1981, Ladder Company No. 4 was decommissioned. On July 14, 1983, Ladder Company No. 3 was decommissioned. On January 1, 2001, Engine Company No. 3 was decommissioned and redesignated Ladder Company No. 3. On January 20, 2001, Engine Company No. 8 was decommissioned and redesignated Ladder Company No. 4. On June 27, 2008, Rescue Company No. 1 was decommissioned.

The question of whether there are a sufficient number of firefighters on duty may be understood by the following. With the decommissioning of Ladder Company No. 5, there was a reduction of four on-duty firefighters. Concurrent with the decommissioning of Engine Company No. 2, there were firefighter layoffs.

The decommissioning of Ladder Company No. 4 and Ladder Company No. 3 resulted in a reduction of on-duty firefighters. Twelve firefighter positions were eliminated in 2008. When the heavy Rescue Company was decommissioned, it was followed months later by nine firefighter layoffs.

The on-duty strength each day is thirty firefighters, excluding the Air Rescue Station and the Marine Unit. Recommended staffing for Ladder No. 4 and Ladder No. 3 is five firefighters. Recommended staffing for Engines 1, 4, 5, 6, 9 and 11 and Ladders 1 and 6 is four firefighters.

Today, there are fewer companies to protect the city and fewer firefighters in the remaining companies. All of these facts closely resemble the events preceding Portland's great conflagration of 1866.

To those more thoughtful guests who ask whether the great conflagration could happen again, we would have to answer, "Yes."

136

NOTES

INTRODUCTION

1. McCarthy, "Portland Water District."
2. Ibid.
3. Chapman, *Conflagration*.
4. *Portland Evening Express*, July 4, 1966.
5. *Portland Daily Advertiser*, July 6, 1866.

FALMOUTH NECK

6. At the foot of India Street.

THE SECOND CONFLAGRATION

7. Deering Oaks Park.

ENJIN AND OPPOSITION

8. Engine was spelled enjin, enjine, engine and ingin in various English and American documents of the time.

9. *Book of Old Falmouth Records*, 304.
10. Willis, *History of Portland*, 519.

LIBERTY AND REBIRTH

11. *Falmouth Gazette*, November 19, 1785. Research by M. Daicy.
12. *Cumberland Gazette*, August 28, 1788.

PORTLAND FIRE DEPARTMENT

13. Fire enjins were referred to as "hand tubs" or "tubs."
14. The term "run" described running to the alarm with the enjin. Today, alarms answered by a company are referred to as runs.
15. In this context, the term "leading" rhymes with "seeding."
16. Foreman or director is the term for captain.

STEAM AGE

17. Actually, over the decades between 1769 and 1883, twenty-seven hand engines—and between 1859 and 1909, twenty-three steam fire engines— were purchased and worked in Falmouth Neck/Portland. The apparatus and companies enumerated in this text are cited because of their historical background and/or impact on the conflagration.

RECOMMENDATIONS AND REJECTIONS

18. John Neal (1793–1876). Portland lawyer, writer, critic, poet, boxer, women's rights advocate and architect.
19. "Wet" is to pump water.

Fire!

20. William W. Ruby, who discovered the fire, was later elected to Steam Fire Engine Machigonne Company No. 1. In 1886, he was elected captain, and in 1888, he was elected assistant engineer.
21. This report, including the strategy to cut off the advance of the massive fire, disproves the line: "The department was an ill trained volunteer staff." Indeed, the Portland firemen were not volunteer but were paid per each alarm to which they responded.
22. "Playing" means pumping.
23. This belies the false accusation that "the fire walked on unchecked."
24. "Pipe" refers to the nozzle.

The Disaster and the Results

25. Low tide. Hard suction was unable to reach water to draft.
26. PVFA Clipping Book, PVFA 0202927252000.
27. Frank Merrill was a member of Machigonne Steam Fire Engine Company No. 1 and chief engineer from 1874 to 1877. He was appointed a member of the Portland Police Department. Officer Merrill died in the line of duty, performing police duties at Box 2-61 for 54 York Street, July 28, 1902.

BIBLIOGRAPHY

Abbott, Jacob. Article. *Maine Normal* 1, no. 2 (January 1867).
————. Article. *Maine Normal* 1, no. 4 (March 1867).
Company Logs: SFE Co. Cumberland No. 3; SFE Co. Casco No. 5; SFE Portland No 2; Chief Engineer's Alarms; Washington Hook & Ladder No. 1. Portland Fire Museum Archives, Portland, ME.
Daicy, Michael. Transcripts. Portland Fire Museum Archives, Portland, ME.
Eastern Argus, June 15, 1867.
Elwell, Edward H. "Portland and Vicinity, 1881." Portland Fire Museum Archives, Portland, ME.
Insurance Services Office, Municipal Survey Service. *Report on Portland, Maine*, February 1973.
National Board of Fire Underwriters, Committee on Fire Prevention and Engineering Standards. *Report on the City of Portland Maine*, March 1950; Supplementary Report August 1958.
Neal, John. "Account of the Great Conflagration in Portland, 1867." Portland Fire Museum Archives, Portland, ME.
Portland Auditor's Report, 1868–69; 1869–70. City of Portland, Portland, ME.
Portland Daily Advertiser, July 6, 1866.
Portland Daily Press, July 6, 1866; July 7, 1866; July 31, 1866.
Portland Fire Department Annual Reports, 1861–62; 1865–66; 1866–67. Portland Fire Museum Archives, Portland, ME.
Portland Press Herald, 1966.
Portland Sunday Press and Times

Portland Water District: A Century of Experience. Portland, ME: Portland Press Herald, March 2008.

PVFA 1002 Clippings Book. Portland Fire Museum Archives, Portland, ME.

Record Books of Old Falmouth. City of Portland archives, Portland, ME.

Werner, William. "Notes on Boston Fire Alarm, 1852–1964" Albert K. Bowers Jr. collection, 1965.

Whitney, Donald Patrick. *Portland Fire Department: A Historian's View.* N.p., 1990.

ABOUT THE AUTHORS

Michael Daicy has been a Portland firefighter since 1983. He has been assigned at Engine Company No. 11 in the East Deering section of the city, where he has served for the last twenty years. Michael has done extensive research on the Portland Fire Department's history. Since 1989, he has been appointed by four fire chiefs as the official department historian. He has built an extensive fire department historical database and produced numerous articles for magazines, newspapers and other publications, which included a 1994 commemorative book on the department. He has also served as editor of the fire department's annual report since 1997. The text of *Portland's Greatest Conflagration* is heavily weighted by these cited works.

Daicy's family genealogy includes Rufus King, one of the signers of the Constitution, and Maine's first governor, William King. Also, Michael has three ancestors who were Portland firemen in the mid-nineteenth century and may have assisted in fighting this great conflagration.

Donald Whitney retired as a lieutenant from the Portland Fire Department and serves as Portland Fire Museum curator. He is an adjunct professor at Southern Maine Community College, Fire Science Department, teaching the history course "Fire in American Society," which he developed. He has authored four books on the Portland Fire Department and has written for national trade magazines.

Visit us at
www.historypress.net